YOU SOLD YOUR COMPANY

Get Ready for Change

J. TED OAKLEY

RIVER GROVE
BOOKS

Published by River Grove Books
Austin, TX
www.rivergrovebooks.com

Distributed by River Grove Books

Design and composition by Greenleaf Book Group and Mimi Bark
Cover design by Greenleaf Book Group and Mimi Bark

Publisher's Cataloging-in-Publication data is available.

Print ISBN: 978-1-63299-597-1

eBook ISBN: 978-1-63299-598-8

First Edition

To Nancy, Keys and Mackenzie,
Sarah and Clint, Frank and Phoebe
All good friends

Why Listen to Ted Oakley?

As a business owner you ask the question—why take advice from this guy? He doesn't have an Ivy League degree. He doesn't have a big Wall Street firm after his name.

Maybe that's exactly why. Because, just like you probably did, I made my own way. I grew up extremely poor. No indoor plumbing, no running water other than a pump on the porch. Even as a small child, I could see that if I wanted something in this world, I was going to have to earn it on my own. I got my first job at age six and always worked from then on. I bought my own clothes and shoes. When I needed a car, I earned the money and bought one. I left home at 18 and made my way, the hard way: one step, one dollar, one class, and one life lesson at a time.

I worked my way through college. I paid my dues in the US

Army. And then I set my sights on the business world. Since those early days, I have started companies, sold companies, and merged companies. I know what it's like to begin at zero, to struggle to meet payroll, and to work 100 hours a week to build a business. Preservation of capital had to be at the front of my mind all the time. And that experience allows me to truly understand the sacrifices most of us who have founded and sustained businesses know are necessary to succeed.

My advice . . . don't let Wall Street thieves, deal makers, and smooth-talking salespeople take it from you. I've been *there* before.

Oxbow Advisors

At Oxbow Advisors, we've spent 35 years working with people who have gained significant first-generation wealth and are trying to maximize it across future generations.

Many of these individuals have experienced liquidity events, and they depend on our extensive knowledge to help them navigate the next steps that will lead to lasting cross-generational wealth.

What we do is simple but hard to find in today's investment world: We protect the wealth you worked hard to create.

If you would like more information, call 512-386-1088 or visit OxbowAdvisors.com

Contents

Introduction

In 1983, I met a business owner who'd recently sold a company—one who would help put me on the trajectory of a lifelong study of and fascination with people in that position. I was intrigued by the whole situation—by the exact and defined business style of this person, by the anything-can-happen moment he was having, and by the rare financial event he'd just undergone: cashing out the company that had been his life's work for a staggering amount of liquid wealth. This was a man who, like me, had come into industry with very little. He'd worked tirelessly to build something substantial. His business had been his baby—one in which he'd invested attachment, pride, worry, devotion, and endless work. His story was punctuated with moments where he acknowledged he'd made it, but he'd had low and hard times along the way. He had sacrificed time and again for his success. Making it, in this case, meant nothing less than fully achieving the American dream—founding a company, creating an economy, supporting employees, engaging the community, and creating a financial legacy not just for one generation but also for the children and grandchildren.

As I write these pages nearly 40 years on, I can tell you that the nature of many of the businesses I see selling has changed, the economy has changed, and the sums of money changing hands in these transactions have exploded. But the owners' attitudes toward the deals that relieve them of the companies they built and sold? The emotions of it all? Those haven't really changed at all. Every owner who goes through this process winds up standing in the same shoes, looking out at an uncertain future, feeling some mix of accomplishment and excitement and also emptiness and uncertainty as one great story of their lives comes to a close and a new one begins.

This group of people—business owners in the midst of making the most consequential financial decisions of their lives—would eventually become a core focus of my work. Meeting their needs would be a primary objective of Oxbow Advisors, the company I founded over 20 years ago in Austin, Texas (about as far from the manipulation and corruption I'd witnessed on Wall Street as I could get). These successful entrepreneurs would become great teachers for me as I learned more from them with each passing year. I would develop a deep and abiding respect for them and for the unique challenges they face as they shift their energies from building a company to managing tremendous wealth. Along the way, I would become an expert in helping this group meet their specific and unusual investment criteria—ensuring long-term security while figuring out what next steps and future ventures are worth their time and resources. And all the while, they're figuring out what fulfillment looks like after every imaginable business goal has been ticked off the list and all of that is in the rearview mirror.

When listening to the general public speak of "business owners" or "bosses," I am always surprised at how little they really know about the business owner. This entrepreneurial group of people is often misunderstood. Owners and former owners of businesses are the lifeblood of this country. They take the most risks, pay the most taxes, and help the most people. Most of them are, at their core, benevolent and philanthropic. Who funds most of the charities and endowments in this country? Business owners and those who sold their companies. The desire to give back is paramount and almost universally shared. In the American economy, these are the people who bring the most to the table—and the reach of their accomplishments goes far beyond money.

Even with all that, they often receive negative media coverage and are among the least appreciated in our society. They get beat up by the government. They get maligned as greedy fat cats who are out for themselves. If you're a business owner who's ever been wrongly painted with this brush, you know those accusations are a bitter pill to swallow. You know you're more and better than that.

UNEXPECTED POTHOLES AND CURVES

This book is designed to take you through a timeline beginning with the day you sell your company. Whether you sold for $5 million or $200 million, I believe this information will benefit your thought processes. The road you take after the sale is going to have some unexpected curves and some unanticipated emotions. Much to the surprise of most business owners who go through this process, it's not all upside. Many do not realize until after the sale how much the business has become a part of them, how much their identity is tied up with it. Few anticipate that when they pull the company they've worked on for ages out of their lives, out of their souls, it leaves behind a sizable hole.

The changes that take place after selling a business can only be experienced. I have counseled more than 3,000 business owners who knew little of what emotions to expect. They had to experience them firsthand. There's no way to skip through this process altogether, but I hope this book will shorten the time span between selling the business and getting on with the next phase of your life.

The examples shared in these pages are real people, though I have changed their names and occasionally identifying details of their businesses. These individuals range among 40 states and almost 100 different kinds of businesses. They include people who lost their fortunes, people who figured out how to live fully and happily after the sale, and those who went on to achieve even greater wealth and professional success. They include those who were miserable with regret and those who were satisfied and happy. It may be a valuable exercise to see if you recognize any of your own potential weaknesses and strengths in their experiences.

As you go forward, remember to be thankful that you are part of this unique group of people. The thrill of being able to both build and sell a business is experienced by only a tiny percentage of the population. As you cross the threshold from owning a business to selling it and go through the changes that follow, I congratulate you on your success.

Finally, it is with great pleasure that I bring you this newly revised edition of my 1998, 2003, and 2012 book of the same title. Whether you're coming to it as an entrepreneur who's spent 40 or 50 years building a small enterprise into an industry force, a game changer who took a mom-and-pop venture and grew it into a big business, or one of the many young visionaries we're seeing these days who nurtured an innovative idea into a fledgling company that some corporate giant had to possess at any cost, I hope you'll find advice that resonates with you in these pages.

CHAPTER 1

Closing Day

You just signed the papers for selling your company. By tomorrow morning the cash will be in your bank. You pause to reflect on how it all began and how it came to an end.

You could be the person in California who borrowed $25,000 on credit cards to start a business that is now worth $25 million. You could be the person who bought a small company from their dad and built it into a $100 million enterprise. You could be the hourly worker who decided to do it on their own and ended up with $5 million.

The stories tend to be similar. The players change, and the sizes of the companies vary. One thing, however, remains constant: Great feelings of accomplishment are soon interrupted. The crew from the acquiring company arrives to take over: the law-yers, the CPAs, and the young MBAs. Then they start telling you what will be happening. "This is your new regional manager." "We've decided to move your office down the hall." "We're going to implement a new billing system." "We're going to change the way we service accounts."

Even if you made a clean break and are watching from a dis-tance, your reactions to early changes likely range from "Was this the right thing to do?" to "What on earth is going on?" to "I feel like an orphan."

How did you end up here? Why did you even sell? You were probably motivated by one of three things: succession, expansion, or profit (or perhaps a combination of these).

MOTIVATOR #1: SUCCESSION

The lack of a clear successor is one of the primary reasons for selling. A parent realizes the children are not interested in run-ning the business. Or the owner has no children or people in the company who are capable of running it. The business must be sold while the owner is still in full command in order to benefit the most. If you sold for any of these reasons, my hat's off to you. Most business owners, like people from all walks of life, have their biggest blind spots when it comes to family. It takes a deeply hon-est assessment to be able to recognize if and when your offspring may be unwilling or unable to run your company for the long term. The point of knowing when both you and your heirs will be better off without your business in the picture is a clear-eyed and sometimes difficult place to reach.

If you're struggling to make peace with your decision, take heart in the fact that in all my years of counseling business owners, many of the most heartbreaking moments have come to those who could not do what you have done. There is nothing sadder than seeing one of Dad and Mom's precious children run the company they built over their lifetimes into the ground—nothing, that is, except the family strife that inevitably comes with the failure. The children blame the parents, blame each other, and blame the company itself. It's impossible to look at these families and not think that each generation would have been better off if the parents had made the hard decision to sell instead.

I'm not saying every owner should sell rather than let the company move down through generations—that is certainly not the case. But I do believe that if your gut told you the wise choice was selling instead of handing the company over to the kids, you were probably right.

MOTIVATOR #2: EXPANSION

A second reason is the inability to gain capital for expansion. Almost every successful business reaches this fork in the road eventually. The owner can overcome the capital problem at certain times, but then the risk becomes too great of losing it all just to grow. A lot of people make the decision to sell then. If the owner sees consolidation in the industry and waits too long, the price goes down. If they see consolidation coming and sell too soon, money is left on the table.

MOTIVATOR #3: PROFIT

The third reason for selling is simply because the offering price is too high to resist. Most business owners know what their companies are worth. They may even know that within a certain time frame the business will likely start to decline. If someone offers more than the business is worth under any circumstances, the owner usually feels they "have to" sell. This is especially true when public stock companies come calling. And if two or three are bidding against each other, the price can go so high it's ridiculous.

Almost every successful company is destined to sell at some point, either to a buyer or to the public market. Like acorns growing on oak trees, then falling to earth where another tree sprouts, everything has a cycle.

Most business owners tend to be blind to the future after selling. In the majority of cases, they have spent the last 10–25 years of their lives focused on running a company. Once the ink dries on the bill of sale, though, they are at a new beginning. This is a watershed event, a turning point—and life after the sale is new territory. This book offers a bit of insight into what this territory will be like. Nobody can provide you with a detailed map—the experience is too individual for that. But as someone who's been through the process alongside thousands of business owners, I can warn you about many of the peaks and valleys you'll have to cross before you get to your new normal on the other side.

Over the years, I've found that business owners seem to have more guts and less fear than individuals lacking the entrepreneurial spirit and drive. They've also got more focus, determination, and self-confidence. But when they sell their companies, they also sell a lot of their power. One critical question is *Can they live with that?*

When they can't—when they can't make peace with the fact that some replacement executive is sitting in their office (likely managing it less efficiently than they did), and that the phone isn't ringing, and that nobody's asking them for direction and decisions—well, that's when they get into trouble.

OXBOW NOTE

If you are a first-generation wealth earner who's just sold your company, this is a critical time in your financial life and an area of specialization for us at Oxbow Advisors. For free copies of more of our books about this make-or-break time, contact us at OxbowAdvisors.com.

CHAPTER 2

The New Routine

The new routine brings major adjustments for the former business owner. At first, this period may feel like a honeymoon. Much time is spent getting to know all the players from the acquiring company in lunches, sessions, and meetings, with nothing particularly notable to determine. Everyone's best foot is being put forward, and potential conflicts are being minimized. The new company may be introducing its acquisition as a new great addition. The former owner probably senses, even this early, that problems could arise, but the honeymoon feeling causes them to believe it'll all work out.

Most business owners are by nature optimistic. They have a tendency in the early months after the sale to assume the kinks will iron themselves out. For this reason, the owner might think,

We'll discuss the problems and find solutions or *I'll compromise a little*. Sometimes this is the case, but, more often than not, what the former owner detects are subtle changes in management style and direction that are likely to get more overt in the weeks and months to come.

This period when there's some semblance of the old routine brings changes one after another. Most of the perks of owning a business start to vanish. Company-paid insurance, car washes and maintenance, errands, cleanups, parties, trips, and phone contracts are just a few of the extras to go. These changes impact the spouse as well, especially if the spouse was used to having many costs and odd jobs absorbed by the company.

Losing fringe benefits pales in comparison to the next blow to the former business owner's routine. When the meetings are over, when the transition is through, when they wake up in the morning and don't have a company to manage, it usually takes about four days for the thud to happen. That's the moment when the owner looks around and thinks, *What have I done?* and *Was this a mistake?*

Most of the time it was not, but it sure can feel that way as you make the transition.

Morris was an owner in the Midwest who sold his business in the early 1980s. I met with him soon after the sale, and he had an upbeat attitude about how everything was going to be great. The acquiring company had promised him the option to expand the business and do well for himself. Each time I visited him after, however, Morris had become less and less enthusiastic.

I have a standard warning to business owners: If you sell your company and agree to be employed by the acquiring company, don't be overly optimistic. Eight out of 10 times it doesn't work. Morris was in this situation and failed to recognize it. After the initial phase wore off, he was shocked. Fifteen months later he was in Florida, with only a vague understanding of how things had gone wrong.

The new routine impacts your customers also. They see the announcement and notice the transfers to different bank accounts. Many of them appear to be shaken, so you assure them that nothing will change. You are trying to convince yourself and them that this is true—but instinctively you know it's not. After all, no one can take care of your customers the way you do. This is precisely why you have done so well.

The new routine is getting established while your primary asset (cash or stock) is sitting there doing nothing. You figure this major reinvestment problem can be taken care of later. Maybe it can; maybe it can't.

If there's one thing I've learned about routine over decades of watching this process play out for one business owner after another, it's this: Make sure you create one. Make a plan for your first few months that's primarily focused on keeping your options open and keeping up your connections. Under no circumstances should you let your relationships go away—not with people in the company who matter to you, not with your vendors you've built connections to, not with consultants who've been important to you. You are in a thinking and growing phase, not a staring-at-the-walls phase. In the beginning of this new part of your life, your new company is you and your family and your assets. How you're going to nurture and grow those things will work itself out in time, but while you're adjusting to life after running your business, set lunches, make plans, and keep up your relationships.

CHAPTER 3

Life after Selling

M ost business owners feel at least somewhat lost after selling their company, a very normal reaction. Assuming "ex"
or "former" status and moping around, trying to figure
out what to do with yourself in the days immediately after selling, seems to be standard operating procedure. From my years of
experience, I can offer several recommendations that might help
smooth this adjustment.

RECOMMENDATION #1: ADOPT A REALISTIC AND PRAGMATIC ATTITUDE

Yes, you were successful—perhaps very successful—in founding
and managing one or more business enterprises and coping with a

variety of financial, marketing, and other challenges. The emphasis here is on the past tense. There is no guarantee that you will succeed in other entrepreneurial/investment undertakings in the future. Business owners as a group, most of whom possess healthy egos, seldom consider failure to be an option. Soon after the sale is finalized, some have a tendency to act impulsively to organize or gain control of another company in services, marketing, or manufacturing—without adequate financial backup or the expertise to make it prosper. These knee-jerk financial decisions have significant potential for disaster. I can't tell you how many times I've encountered people who made this mistake because they were blind to what could happen, to the fact that it's actually easy to lose $20 million or $40 million through impetuous, overconfident actions.

This doesn't mean that former owners shouldn't look for other businesses, but you must be patient, patient, patient. Your friends and family will likely be asking, "So now what are you going to do with your life?" Most of the time the answer should simply be "I haven't decided yet." Relish this time when you have infinite possibilities. That in itself is a luxury. An optimal choice with an excellent reward-to-risk ratio will eventually appear, and if you've been slow and deliberate in this process, you'll recognize it.

Examples of two individuals who sold their businesses, then reacted in different ways, come to mind. Chuck sold a company in the Southeast and immediately decided to go out and buy a

NASCAR racing company. He had never been in the racing business and merely enjoyed the sport. Over the next three years he lost his entire nest egg and wasn't able to make his racing business successful. He had been set for life but is now back working again in order to make it.

Tim, on the other hand, sold his company to a public corporation and waited until an ideal situation presented itself. He moved slowly and, within two years, started a new company somewhat related to his old one. Another two years later, he has an organization that is larger than the original. Tim is still expanding, and he's happy with how it all came together.

There were a number of key differences in the ways these two former business owners proceeded, but the most consequential were patient, thoughtful progression and choosing a business relevant to experience. Chuck went the wrong way on both counts. First, he should have bided his time and done his homework. Second, if he was determined to invest in an industry about which he knew virtually nothing (aka a hobby), he should have started small. He could have hired someone in the industry to show him the ropes for a year. He could have made a small trial investment. There were no reasons to go all in except his impatience and his ego.

Chuck is not the only one. I've seen former business owners make this mistake in as many ways as you can imagine—buying a boat company, buying a winery, buying a hotel somewhere they like to vacation. That tendency for former business owners to feel like they've got the Midas touch, like they can't possibly lose—that's something I've seen a new example of every year for as long as I've been in finance. There is no amount of money you can't lose with that attitude. In fact, there may be nothing more financially dangerous than thinking you can do no wrong.

RECOMMENDATION #2: SET UP AN OFFICE AWAY FROM HOME

Get a real office! After 10, 20, or more years with the company, the business owner who liquidates is without management responsibility—but typically brings all of the office paraphernalia home anyway. Most families aren't set up for this, and most families don't like it. The spouse who's been on the job 10 or 12 hours a day for decades suddenly trying to find purpose behind a slew of computer monitors on the dining room table? Not a welcome sight for anyone in the family. It's not satisfying for anyone involved.

A better option is to lease a space and set up a desk, a table, and a few bookshelves. Establish a schedule that brings you there at least a couple days a week (or every morning if that's what you need to make this transition).

The greatest benefit of an office for a former owner may well be quiet time. You are at a point where reflection on your life and situation is important. Having both a place to go and a routine is healthy after selling.

RECOMMENDATION #3: DON'T SUDDENLY BECOME A PROFESSIONAL INVESTOR

Just because a newly acquired fortune provides easy access to stock, bond, real estate, and option and derivative markets, the former owner doesn't automatically qualify as a great investor. As I write these pages, the financial world is in a situation where we've had a good market with only a couple major hiccups (case in point, spring of 2020) for the better part of 12 years. Because of this, many investors, especially young ones, have never experienced a bad market. They've seen steady gains on everything they've touched. It's been a great time to be an investor, but anyone who's lived in this world long enough can tell you that even the best markets come to an end. I had people in 2000 who'd been day trading for a couple years, winning every day, and I watched them lose almost everything. The kind of explosive and illogical growth I've seen since in the markets dwarfs the late 90s boom. There are companies that don't make any money and yet their stocks soar. It is just a matter of time until, to paraphrase Warren Buffet, the tide goes out and we discover who's been swimming naked.

James was a good friend and client who turned to day trading almost immediately after selling his company. He became, overnight, an investment business. The problem? He actually knew very little about investing. He seemed to forget that investing is a unique sphere with many risks along with its rewards. In the beginning, he traded, bought, and sold like it was a full-time vocation.

When I visited him the next year, I asked how his investments were faring. His reply was that he was done with them. After some painful lessons, James had come to realize that his task was to determine how much of his money to allocate to various types of investment vehicles, making sure he understood the risks. Having done that, he also knew that his area of expertise lay not in making money by investing but in finding capable money managers on whom he could depend to help him reach his goals.

Passive investing through professional managers can look like an easy and simple solution. In reality, however, investing assets is a much slower process than most people think. Of course, patience is important, but it's only one of many prerequisites in this increasingly complex and constantly changing field. Former owners interested in active investments are strongly advised to wait for the right business to come along. Their prior experience will then prove valuable in making a wise selection.

RECOMMENDATION #4: BE CAREFUL WHO YOU LISTEN TO

Investing in a new business requires tedious and detailed scrutiny of the target. If you start calling a number of business friends and deal makers looking for a place to put your money, the people on the other end of those calls will be all too happy to help. Corporate-finance people and deal makers will suddenly proliferate like dandelions in the springtime. People who've made money (even if by accident) and those who dream of it show up with "great," "can't fail" opportunities. As you hear these people out, rest assured that the best investors I've observed decade after decade are extremely slow to commit capital. They wait. They study. They know the players and they know the facts. They never blindly put their money into a stranger's hands.

After the sale of the business is a time for former owners to listen. Their best opportunities are more likely to come from being around known business professionals than around people who've come out of the woodwork with investment suggestions. You'd do well to stay close to active business owners in as many areas of operations as possible. Those corporate officers are often the first to learn when a business is going to be on the block. Potential buyers who were former owners won't want to overlook any enterprise available for purchase that has potential. Sure, look at everything, but take the time to watch carefully and to stay in tune with related economic and financial developments.

CHAPTER 4

Reality Check

Reality after the sale of a business comes in different packages. The business owner who stays with the new company has one type of new reality, the business owner who retires (or tries to) has another, and the individual who owns multiple companies generally experiences very little change after selling just one.

The business owner who stays with the company usually takes a needed vacation, pays off debt, and/or contemplates next steps, all the while trying to adjust to the next reality. I'm amazed at how many business owners are surprised that the marriage of the two companies seldom goes as planned. Big corporations usually buy smaller companies in order to control, grow, and run their new entities. They bought; you sold! Very few corporations are run well enough to allow the prior owner to join in the decision-making (growth) phase. Too many egos, too much power, too many bean counters for that.

ENTREPRENEURIAL COMPANIES VS. CORPORATIONS

Most entrepreneurial companies are more efficiently run than large or even medium-sized corporations. Generally speaking, among the top executives of these corporations, few, if any, have ever been threatened seriously by financial insecurity, had to meet payroll, or had to "mortgage their soul" to make something happen. Very few executives have faced day-to-day fear of losing it all in the workplace. The differences between entrepreneurs who risk everything to build their companies and people who are high-level employees at big companies run deep, and they show up as big and small decisions are being made about how the company you founded is going to be run under the new ownership.

Lloyd was a client and former owner who sold to a public company. When we first started working together, he was jubilant about the prospects of the new combination. I told him to be circumspect because his company might have been managed more efficiently and cost-effectively than the larger acquiring company could maintain. He was a great operator, and sure enough, the executive controllers of the mother company gave every indication of being afraid of him. From the standpoint of corporate powerbrokers at the new headquarters he was serving, Lloyd was a potential problem more than he was a potential partner. The new owners wanted to prove themselves different and better, and they wanted to do it under their own steam. As it happened, the company made one misstep after another until they developed severe financial problems, and Lloyd wisely left.

SIGNS OF STRESS

As part of their reality check, most former business owners who stay on with the new corporation begin to experience signs of stress. Here are three examples:

Sign #1: Accounting and procedure changes

Some of the loyal employees of the former owner come along with him—and they are soon being driven crazy by all the updated procedures enforced by the new home office. It may be that a 30-year-old MBA with the new company starts insisting every requisition form has to be approved at regional headquarters. It may be the new regime starts lengthening accounts payable, shortening accounts receivable, or piling on new accounting charges. It may be that when they're under pressure to scare up money at the end of the quarter, they do financial gymnastics like recategorizing expenses. One of the biggest problems here, aside from the time and energy staff start spending on all of this, is that this new system is focused on *showing* money on the books today. In process after process, they're not even thinking about revenue. At best they're just trying to paint a picture of profit.

Sign #2: The new company doesn't keep old promises

As a business owner you likely had strong feelings about how to manage and support employees and how to treat customers and business associates. Chances are you built relationships with all these connections over years, maybe over decades. Some of those relationships became personal. All of them mattered to you on some level.

One of the hardest things for a former business owner to witness is any denigration of those relationships. When an executive who worked for you is demoted or chooses to jump ship because the new leadership doesn't value their contributions, it hurts. When you run into customers and hear they're dissatisfied, it's infuriating. You built these connections, and the new company may be slowly (or even quickly) eroding them.

Very few circumstances provide such a powerful reality check as to how much things have changed since you were running the business—even if you've still got an office with your name on the door.

Sign #3: When the former owner's ideas aren't valued

The operating systems of large corporations don't adjust easily to conducting business on anything other than a grand scale. At best, the former owner is likely to be patronized or treated condescendingly. At worst, they're ignored. This is a shift that happens remarkably quickly for a lot of sellers. One day they're being courted to sell, invited to be a part of the new regime, wined and dined and treated with the highest regard.

A few weeks later, the sale is done, the decisions are coming from corporate headquarters, the company's culture is already shifting, and nobody in a position of authority wants to hear cautions, concerns, or contributions from the former owner.

My advice on this is simple. If you maintain a role with the company, be prepared for it, and have an exit strategy that gives you a clean break. Sometimes the best thing you can do at this juncture is walk away.

I find it fascinating that some of the most successful company sales for all parties go an entirely different way from what's described in these points. In a minority of cases, the buying corporation stays mindful that they want the company because it's already successful. For example, when Warren Buffett buys a company, he typically evaluates the private enterprise, its philosophy, values, and returns. If it's all working, he doesn't change the sign out front, doesn't change the accounting, doesn't change the leadership. What he wants is an annual return on his investment. In a case like that, the whole point of the sale is to see a successful company continue to succeed. It's a smart, but rare, way to do it.

THE PERILS OF CONSULTANCY

When a corporation buys a company, it invariably has an agenda. The former owner is put into a so-called consulting role for one of three reasons:

Reason #1: It's part of the price of the buyout

This often takes place because more money is needed to close the transaction. The former owner in reality does little or no consulting. As a matter of fact, the acquiring company usually doesn't even bother to call. People ask what the founder is doing, and the euphemism "consulting" pops up.

Reason #2: The acquiring company doesn't want to ruffle feathers

The buyers really don't want or plan to keep the former owner, but they have difficulty saying so. Customarily the main goals of the acquiring company are to get the deal underway and make a smooth transition. In that scenario, the former owner is just a footnote.

Robert was a business owner who lived in the Midwest but sold his company to a publicly owned concern in Texas. He was classified as a consultant, as well as a director. In many public companies, power and politics are even more important, surprisingly, than making money. This was the case with Robert and the acquiring company. After four or five board meetings, he realized that "consulting" meant next to nothing. It soon became evident that the new owners were never going to listen to him or change their ideas on any subject. At the beginning of the second year, the company bought out his contract, and he left.

I'm also reminded of Scotty in Tennessee whose business was acquired by a public company. The buyers wanted him to consult with their merger/acquisition manager when potential new companies were being acquired. After Scotty visited two of the potential acquisition candidates, he concluded that they should not be bought because of a lack of quality in many areas. This counsel, however, put the merger/acquisition manager in an awkward position. Three months later Scotty's contract was purchased, and he was a consultant no more.

Reason #3: The former owner is there to retain top customers

Paula owned a business in Denver that was sold to a public company. She had three clients who represented a large portion of her service business. The acquiring company made her a consultant in order to keep these customers. The former owner had no office, only her home. But when two of the three customers left, the acquiring company also said goodbye to Paula.

Consulting tends to be very hard for the former business owner. They are neither in nor out but usually in an ambiguous and temporary limbo. If a business owner sells the firm and works directly for the new company, the number one rule is clear:

Do what upper management tells you to do. This is usually a managerial assignment, not a consulting position. In some cases, the former owner's status is actually much clearer by being an employee instead of a consultant. One thing is certain: The new company will run operations differently than the original owner did, and that can be hard to watch.

The former owner is advised to keep consulting in perspective and negotiate the most favorable financial terms for the contract. At best, consulting is a stopgap measure before doing something else. The period spent at this position may be one to three years, but eventually—in almost all cases—the former owner moves on, either by choice or by the decision of the new management. Consulting for the new company nearly always looks better on paper than it is in reality.

OXBOW NOTE

If you recently sold your business, you're as vulnerable to wealth loss as you'll ever be in your life. For a free copy of my book Danger Time: The Two-Year Red Zone after Selling Your Company *and more books and videos on this subject, visit OxbowAdvisors.com.*

CHAPTER 5

Family Relationships after the Sale

People tend to think of family and business as separate entities, but when you own the business, when you built it, your family's fortunes are closely tied to it—and not just in terms of money. Most owners who sell underestimate just how much of an impact the sale will have on the people they love. This is a subject that requires your attention before, during, and after closing day.

One big factor in your family's adjustment depends on which family members were involved in the business. In the event it was built and managed by a married team—with the principal owner working full time and the other spouse at a 50% or higher level—a unique family problem may arise. If the buyer retains the former owner in some capacity, this is usually the only contract signed with the new management. The spouse who is turned away generally receives no monetary compensation or other recognition of their contributions. A radically altered lifestyle inevitably unfolds for this couple. To what extent they enjoy the changes depends on each specific situation and, of course, their personalities.

Jeff and Bonnie were a couple in the West who had a thriving niche business. When their company was purchased, the acquiring corporation kept Jeff but not Bonnie. In many ways Bonnie had been the guiding force in this company, the person to whom most of the employees turned for guidance. She was essential to the business's success and also to its acquisition.

The offering price was so generous that neither Bonnie nor Jeff felt they could turn it down. Unfortunately, the business faltered after the changeover. The new owners never identified the reason. It wasn't such a mystery to those of us who'd had a close relationship with this business before the sale. Had the buyers retained Bonnie's services as well as Jeff's, the company would probably have continued its established pattern of earnings growth.

COMPLICATIONS OF ADULT CHILDREN IN THE BUSINESS

The thorniest issues business owners face after a sale involve the children, especially if any of those children are (or were) employed by the company. These are financial issues, but that's the least of it. They are also emotional, often poking at the most sensitive spots in parent-child and sibling relationships. Handling them poorly can lead to heartbreak and a legacy of discontent.

My best advice on this starts with treating your kids equally. There are many ways to calculate things another way—from looking at who needs more to who has earned more to who you think you're most likely to see at the table on Thanksgiving—but the simplest way to be straightforward with your family is equal sharing. This isn't something you can do in a vacuum or from the shadows. Don't just send checks and expect the kids to sort out their feelings among themselves. Talk with them. Let them know what you've done and why and that your choices are made from love.

In many families this will be enough to get things moving forward in a positive direction, but sometimes there are arguments and protests. In some cases you may feel compelled to clarify your decisions. There are a couple of basic explanations that can get you started on the right foot—forthright and caring but not apologetic.

First among these is that the business was yours. Anything you do for your family out of the sale is because you care for them and want to see them prosper. Those gifts are not an entitlement and not a substitute for kids making their own way.

Second, you may have to handle protests from those children who were directly in the business. They are the most likely to cry foul and to think they're being shortchanged. The truth in most families' circumstances is that a child in the business is still someone who was given a job. Most of these individuals were not entrepreneurs. They didn't risk their own necks to build the company. They didn't mortgage the house or lose sleep or forgo their own salary to make payroll. Unless you have an arrangement with a child that specifically creates an ownership position for them, your role should be an emotionally but not financially supporting one as they pursue the next phase of their careers.

In general, the more children who were employed by the company, the greater the potential for problems. If the acquiring company elects not to keep any or all children as employees, new careers must be generated. If the acquiring company chooses to employ only one of the children, this can cause family tensions and discord.

Ben owned a business in the Southeast that employed three of his adult children. All were granted positions with the new company after the sale. Three years later, two of the children had been terminated, and the third was moved to a different site. Ben was disgruntled with the company for breaking up his family work unit. Truth be told, he just hadn't been capable of doing what should have been done in the beginning—not hiring the children when he organized his company, or encouraging them to seek alternative employment at the time of the sale.

Within the home, family members experience a different but related set of issues. When a business owner employs family members, both personal and professional relationships exist. The business can seep into the family hierarchy in many ways. In addition, salaries and draws in the family's private company will be far different from the practices of a publicly traded corporation. When the company is sold, some of the ties that bind these family members together are loosened or severed. This doesn't have to be a bad thing. Your family can reinvent its relationships without the company. Having observed the sale of numerous family businesses, though, I've noted that some families choose to go their separate ways, at least for a while. Each member has his or her own measure of financial independence and wants something different in life. In the long run families have to figure out how things work among them after the company is out of the picture.

KIDS AND THE MOST COMMON MONEY MISSTEP

We all want our children to be self-sufficient, to have integrity, and to have high self-esteem. What many of us don't realize is that they're unlikely to achieve those traits if we lavish them with money from the get-go. Over the years I have counseled many former business owners who just would not listen to sound advice on this. They made all the mistakes: giving the kids too much money too quickly; making them feel rich when they hadn't earned a thing; and taking away their all-important motivation to make their own way.

At the end of the day, most major post-sale family problems arise when the owner of the business tries to financially support other family members—usually adult children. In my opinion, this is a recipe for disaster on multiple levels. Besides the relationship matter at stake, there's also the depletion of assets. If a business owner is trying to support two or three families in addition to their own, the assets will need to be very large. I have witnessed $10 million, $20 million, and more shrink rapidly when three or four families were relying on it for support. And, of course, as the principal shrinks, so does the ordinary income it generates.

Cecil and his wife sold a great business in California and had enough money to last their entire lifetime and more. The cash flow they were generating from investments was large. As they moved along in time, however, each adult child started using Mom and Dad to maintain and improve their lifestyle. Over time, I met on several occasions with the parents in an effort to help them understand that their own lifestyle could be in jeopardy and might ultimately require a radical reduction of these family subsidies. My counsel was ignored, and over the long run, the children squandered most of the balance of the fortune.

This unfortunate result transpired largely because the parents were not able to tell their children, "You need to make your own money and provide for your own financial security and independence." As it played out, the children were robbed of the chance to make it on their own merits, build their self-confidence, and earn respect. In the end, everyone was damaged. This family financial tragedy occurs and reoccurs repeatedly.

So what does the owner do?

If you have children or a spouse in the business, be prepared to address the consequences of selling sooner rather than later. As much as possible, let everyone in the family know how their lives might change after the sale, especially in terms of money. They may or may not have jobs. Their salaries may or may not be the same. If possible, make sure that the mature children know in advance that they will be on their own. This doesn't mean you can't choose to make a gift or help them in some specific way, but it is all too easy for the kids to look over at what's transpired in the business and think that they, too, are set for life when that's not actually the case. If you find these conversations difficult (and most people do), tally the benefits of "tough love." One benefit may be preserving your own new lifestyle. Another will be your mental and emotional health. A more subtle but critical benefit may be helping the kids maintain healthy relationships with money.

Remember as you go through this process that your actions speak as loudly as your words. Keep in mind that if you jump out there and buy a big jet, vacation houses, and a yacht in the first year, rejecting all financial caution and reason, your children will be watching. No matter how old they are, they'll be taking it in. If you throw large sums of money and new luxury perks their way during this same period, you'll be fostering a money-is-nothing-to-me attitude. You worked hard to build your company, and that process taught you to value every resource and appreciate every advantage. So are carelessness, waste, and greed really what you want to teach your children in the end? This first stretch when you're getting accustomed to big changes in your life is the worst possible time to flaunt your wealth. Try to go slow, keep a low profile, and just quietly enjoy your new-found financial freedom.

Does this mean you can't enjoy your fortune or that you can't share it with the kids? Of course not. But do these things in moderation. Keep your priorities in perspective: The happiness and well-being of your family come first. Money is just a single aspect of that, so don't let it become the defining feature.

However you decide to share or not share your wealth with your family, I urge you to make detailed plans with emphasis on how your children fit in. If at all possible, do it well before you're sitting with the money in the bank, making decisions that will have long-term implications.

OXBOW NOTE

Because family is such a critical issue to wealth preservation, at Oxbow we excel not just in helping families with money but in structuring arrangements so that money doesn't disappear in the next generation. For more information about how to approach legacy planning in your own family, contact us at OxbowAdvisors.com. For a specific discussion of raising families who aren't tainted by wealth, you can request a free copy of my book Rich Kids, Broke Kids: The Failure of Traditional Estate Planning.

CHAPTER 6

The Biggest Risk

S oon after selling the company, the former owner enters the riskiest phase of the journey. This period is broken down into two parts: first, the period when the individual has been paid for the sale, and second, the period when the seller is considering other possibilities for investment. Both of these areas can be devastating to the newfound wealth. The first months after the sale are so fraught with mistakes and regrets I've written a separate book about them called *Crazy Time: Surviving the First 12 Months after Selling Your Company*. Feel free to contact us at Oxbow for a copy.

After the company is sold, the former owner has liquidity as never before. In this new status, when plans aren't clear for reinvestment, most owners believe that liquidity makes the situation conservative. They can't lose. What happens now is the need to keep pace with inflation, to conserve assets, and to be very defined. The fact is, they are facing bigger risk than when they owned the business. Remember, there are two kinds of assets for the former owner: base capital and investing capital. Base capital is needed to produce cash flow for a lifestyle, while investing capital is everything that is left over. It's important not to confuse the two. One of them can quietly, gradually be drawn down until you haven't got enough income to support your way of life. The other can quite literally be wiped out overnight. It's critical that you guard against either outcome.

YOU CAN'T CONTROL THE INVESTMENT MARKET

Keeping pace with inflation is a must. Whereas business owners are largely in control of their business, whether good or bad, this new situation involves having liquidity and virtually no control over selected investments. You can't run all those companies you're buying stock in. In fact, you can't run any of them. Explosions of investments tend to happen at this stage, and too often they are poorly chosen without nearly enough investigation. Here's an all-too-familiar report card: bad timing, bad investments, and poor planning. Remember this: You are no longer in control. Everything you do must be thoroughly examined. If you make a mistake, there will be no turning back. When the company was yours, you could bounce back after hard times. But when losses come after selling the business, bouncing back is unlikely. You are now in the big-risk arena, and this is not a situation to be taken lightly.

With those risks in mind, choose an experienced, honest, proven investment expert to guide you through the task at hand: putting your base capital to work to support your lifestyle for the long term. Don't be one of those people who reads an article on Wikipedia or a week's worth of financial papers about investment strategy and thinks they've got it all figured out. This is a mistake I see multiple times every year, and it usually ends with the investor deciding to start over—except at that point they've got less capital with which to work.

In the excitement and the long trend of an "up, up, and away" stock market, sometimes investors lose sight of the number one objective of any investment: maintaining the buying power of your assets. If inflation, for example, is sitting at 4%, you need to earn 6%. You need to cover that gap to generate cash flow and maintain your buying power. That's the game, and it's a methodical one. If you're starting out your new phase of investment thinking it's about searching for the Holy Grail of stock buys, you're going to get yourself into trouble before long.

NO NEED TO DIVE HEADFIRST

The other key aspect of this big-risk time frame is investment in the next business or deal. The vast majority of former owners want to invest in an idea that will make money. That's only natural after their previous success. They thrive on doing the best deal. Most former owners did very well in their own "deal," which is precisely how they got wealthy.

There's an expression that *fools rush in where angels fear to tread*—and, sadly, far too many former business owners fit the description. They jump quickly to the next business without taking the time to examine it in detail. The single most common mistake made by former business owners is moving too quickly. Why the rush? Do you really need more money right away? I doubt it. You must carefully analyze all attractive options available, then take the time to reflect, utilizing sage counsel along the way. Pace yourself and you'll come out ahead.

There are thousands of deals out there that can make or break a former business owner. Someone is always there trying to separate you from your money. People will be selling and pitching to you in one form or another almost daily. Do not respond to any pressure that comes with these dialogues. You have time. You don't have to be in business again immediately. Every salesperson will try to make you think their deal is the very last great opportunity, but rest assured that more deals will come your way. Be patient and enjoy looking at them. You are in control. That control, however, vanishes after the investment is made. Watch and wait. You have time.

How do the miscalculations made during this phase play out in real life? As I write this, I'm less than a month out from watching one of these implosions. James sold the company he'd carefully shepherded for 30 years for $25 million. Within weeks of the funds hitting his accounts, this once careful, deliberate, and extremely successful businessman got swept up in the euphoria and ego trip of it all and broke both of the cardinal rules. First, he bought a massive Southwestern ranch and a private jet and made six-figure gifts to each of his kids (who were barely adults and certainly not ready to manage that kind of cash). That ate up more than one fifth of what should have been his base capital (without it ever making him a dime). Second, he dropped about $7 million in new businesses about which he knew very little. Just like that, half his liquidity was gone. His base capital took a huge hit, and he put a large amount of his wealth into high-risk deals. It had taken James roughly *four weeks* to spend half of what he'd earned with three decades of business building.

The observation of Blaise Pascal, a 17th-century mathematician and philosopher, is appropriate here. He said that most human misfortune stems from "man's inability to sit still in a room." James would surely be in a stronger position today if he could have just sat quietly and given his wisdom a fighting chance to temper his enthusiasm.

OXBOW NOTE

Strange as it may sound, holding on to wealth often turns out to be harder for families than getting it in the first place. The majority of wealthy Americans fail to keep their fortunes in the family for more than a single generation—and many don't make it that far. If you'd like a free copy of The Psychology of Staying Rich: How to Preserve Wealth and Establish an Enduring Financial Legacy, *contact us at OxbowAdvisors.com.*

CHAPTER 7

Emptiness

Business owners often get so caught up in the acquisition deal that just about everything else is forgotten. After all the hype and hoopla of the sale, the business owner walks away with millions. At that point, often for the first time since childhood, they are debt-free, job-free, and responsibility-free.

From the outside, the scenario usually looks like a no-lose situation. The company is sold. With adequate capital for a lifetime of total financial security and freedom, what more could any person ever want? But somewhere in all the excitement and confusion is the heart of the seller. This formerly successful entrepreneur is supposed to be on top of the world, but inside there is often an emptiness, a sudden lack of goals and purpose. The emptiness stems from once having everything to do and suddenly having nothing to do. The contrast between your former life and your present life can be stark. In some ways this stage of life isn't too different from graduating from high school. All your friends are going in different directions, attending different schools, and taking on different jobs. At first, you don't know exactly what you want to do. Somehow you decide—and off to some university or job you go. You're back on track. When you sell your company, most of your friends are still running their businesses, have jobs, and so forth. Somehow you will need to get your bearings in this new situation.

Here's how it plays out in the very grown-up scenario of selling a company: Running your business is like playing a football game. You prep and you work and you bond with your team and you run all your plays. You give it just about everything, body and soul, until you find a way to win in the end. Then, in a blink, it's over. You're not on the team anymore. You don't have to work out. You don't have to practice. You don't have to strategize. You don't even have to get out of bed in the morning if you don't feel like it. You won, and in the moment that was awesome. But after the fact, all you can think is *Now what?*

This kind of life shake-up is bound to impact your social life as well. Up until the sale, there's a good chance you and many of the friends, colleagues, and family members in your life were on parallel paths. Yes, you had a company, but just like everyone else you were working hard to earn every dollar.

Your friends may have the same marital status. Maybe you have kids around the same ages. You may live in the same or similar neighborhoods.

When you sell your company and you cash in $25 million or $50 million or more, there's a shift. There's an essential difference between you and those people now, whether you like it or not. You have the kind of wealth most people only ever dream of, and there's a good chance even people who've known you for decades are in fact still dreaming about it. Relationships shift as a result of this change. They do not have to be ruined by it, but during that initial time, feeling like you're alone in this situation can add to that sense of emptiness.

A CAUTIONARY TALE

Mike was an owner in the Northwest who sold his company and stayed on to run the business. He had only a high school education. He'd worked on that business his entire life, building something productive and important every day. After selling, he became despondent and had tremendous seller's remorse. Running the business for someone else became so frustrating that he eventually quit and moved away. I don't think he was ever truly happy afterward.

Getting out of college sometimes produces a similar feeling. You have reached a level that is supposed to make you and everyone else very happy. But this concept is a tough sell to a graduate who is 23 years old and jobless.

The business owner, after selling, often feels emotionally drained, even depressed. They expected this hour to be a happy one. However, a loss of focus and purpose has occurred, and it's one that often demands a period of mourning. How do you get your groove back? No spouse, second home, unlimited golf, or extended travel will fill the void. This question that's asked over and over again is *Why don't I feel happy?*

Most people *will* feel happy again. This is a stage you need to get through. It's a time to take stock and look inward. A time to ask, *What do I like?* and *How do I want to spend my days?* For some, the sale of a business ushers in the opportunity for a spiritual awakening. For some, it's a time to study and learn. For some, it's a time to mentor someone else or to nurture relationships that have been neglected. For others, the sale signals a seismic shift in focus and energy where what had previously been hobbies and avocations take on a more central role.

During the push and pressure of running a business, there were precious few moments for reflection and contemplation, so be patient with yourself during this time. Don't beat yourself up for not feeling happy all the time. You *did* win the game. Now you have the luxury of figuring out what you want to be great at next.

CHAPTER 8

When You're Ready, Bet on the People

Business owners will often sell one business and, after some time, reinvest in another one. One of the most nagging questions becomes: What level or percentage of their time should they invest in the new business? Another is whether this person who has been 100% in control until now can be comfortable with a smaller role.

For many, the optimal scenario would be to own a company and spend 30% to 50% of their time with the new entity. This would allow the owner to enjoy the fruits from the sale of the first company, have regular involvement in management decisions in a new venture, and have new professional goals to achieve. After toiling for many years to develop, then sell, the first business, the former owner usually doesn't want to become immediately locked full time into another. They also have the option to invest in a company and hire officers to exercise daily oversight—while still retaining chief executive control.

Unfortunately, in the real world, this doesn't usually happen. The once and future business owner knows that things rarely run right—by their standards—without hands-on leadership. When their own money isn't on the line, employees don't usually perform as an owner would. The owner is the boss or not the boss. There isn't much middle ground. If employees know the owner is absentee, that fact has an impact. The organization that was sold had the former owner's style and flavor all over it. In a new, part-time commitment, that presence may not exist, or it may be hard to detect.

Marcos was a client who sold a company in the Southwest and soon after bought another one in California. His idea was to have a corporation providing reasonable income in order to offset incidental expenses—one which would require a limited number of hours and no rigid schedule. When he and I reviewed his new management arrangement, he admitted the upsetting dilemma of entrapment in full-time employment. Within two years Marcos had sold the company and was back to square one. His experience was all too typical.

TWO TYPES OF SITUATIONS
CAN WORK WELL

What does work? Two types of situations come to mind that I've observed to be generally satisfactory.

First, if the former owner had a top-notch, longtime employee who knew the business well, this might be a starting point. Two ingredients must be in place: (1) The employee manager should be in the same type of business in the second venture as in the first, and (2) the employee should own at least a small percentage of the new business. In this manner, the former owner can own controlling interest and not necessarily be there all the time. This can be a great setup.

Allen was a client in the Southeast who sold a company and retired—or so he thought. After searching four years for another business, he was unsuccessful in finding what he wanted. In the meantime, his former top manager and two supervisors contacted him to offer their services in a new business, one essentially the same as the old one. He accepted their proposal, and the business worked like a dream. All the key ingredients were there. Same business, same employees. The only difference was a small investment by the former owner. Allen didn't bet the farm the second time around. He let the new management bear the brunt of corporate expansion.

Second, a situation that sometimes works well is when the former owner invests in two or three companies that he knows well, and then acts as a board member only. This has been a satisfactory arrangement for many investors. If they know the business and the people involved, then it has a chance of working. This allows former owners to invest in multiple companies and still exercise influence on major corporate decisions. If the above conditions do not apply, great caution must be exercised.

Note that each of these scenarios focuses on the people. When choosing a business investment, former business owners will save themselves a lot of trouble if they put at least as much time and energy into choosing the *who* of their next investment as they do on the *what*. Work with people who have proven themselves and earned your trust. They are the key to any kind of success in passive or part-time ownership.

WHEN A PART-TIME ROLE IS NOT ENOUGH

Frank was a client in the Northwest who sold an industrial company and shortly afterward bought another company. He would fly into town and work at the company about a fourth of the time. He became upset when employees didn't know he was the owner—or didn't treat him as such. All they knew was that his full-time manager signed their checks. In their eyes, the manager was the real boss. In theory, the part-time system sounded great, but it didn't work for this former business owner who wanted and needed a central role to feel fulfilled.

Not being 100% involved is difficult for some former business owners, even when the goal was part-time management. For some investor-owners, it has to be full time and full control—or nothing at all. They can't just dip a toe in the water. Typically, the former owner would like to run the business on 20-hour weeks, but many instinctively know that the business world demands more. This actually works out fine for a lot of former owners, who find they are happier if they get back into the saddle on a full-time basis. Running the show is in their blood, and they thrive when they accept that.

This is one more reason why an individual who sells a business should take some time before going on to the next. Carefully consider the level of commitment you want to make and how you can be successful in that scenario.

Lastly, a word to the wise: If the former owner truly wants to *own* another business but is not prepared to put in the requisite time and effort, they should remain retired.

CHAPTER 9

"Have I Got a Deal for You"

One thing is certain for owners after selling their companies: Everyone has a deal for them! Newfound wealth brings out all the deal people. Hype such as "50% on this" and "double your money on that" abounds. Everyone seems to know how best to invest your new wealth. Oddly enough, many former business owners go for this. Having spent their entire work lives building net worth, some recklessly reinvest it in a matter of weeks.

New money will always attract people. Wheelers and dealers, not to mention relatives and friends, will find out about it, no matter how hard the business owner tries to keep news of the sale under their hat. In even the most closely held situations, people still find ways to get in touch, to make a pitch, to send a request. Some of these ways are perfectly aboveboard, but some are pretty underhanded, involving borderline stalking and showing up as if by chance.

After the sale of your company, you don't need to be paranoid, but you do need to be careful. The ways to go about protecting your new wealth, your privacy, and your sanity start with learning to say *no*. As a business owner, you undoubtedly had plenty of practice and could comfortably decline anything you needed to, but this will feel different. Most owners who've recently sold are not yet as comfortable with their ability to manage a giant nest egg as they were with their ability to manage the business. This is all the more reason to be cautious and go into these things planning to refuse.

POLITELY DECLINE MOST LOAN REQUESTS

A word of caution regarding friends and relatives: When they come knocking on the door for loans or advances, know that the results of this kind of lending are often disastrous. Friends and relatives typically pay you back last of all. A family member is easier to borrow from and much less onerous to deal with if the loan or advance goes unpaid. Family gatherings become strained afterward, and often everyone involved comes to regret the transaction.

Most of the time, politely declining is the way to go, but this doesn't mean you can't ever share with the people you care about. It means you should tread carefully, and if there's someone you love who has a small need you want to meet, consider a no-strings-attached gift rather than setting up a loan. In the end, you'll have the satisfaction of a good deed, the person you care about will come out ahead, and neither of you will spend your future years together stewing over who borrowed what and didn't pay it back.

Unfortunately, you will likely also be asked for loans and gifts that are substantial. You'll know they're a bad idea, but you may feel pulled to get involved anyway. Go into these situations prepared to decline. Large gifts, loans, or investments to people in your personal life can easily pile up until they're making a dent in your own financial health and upsetting the balance in your relationships.

BE EVEN MORE GUARDED TOWARD BUSINESS PROPOSALS

Once the news of your sale comes out, dealing with requests from friends and family members will likely just be a warm-up for what you'll face from strangers. There's something about a newly minted multimillionaire that makes a lot of unscrupulous people think they've found a gullible mark. You'll be approached from every angle, but one of the most popular is the "What's a million to you when you could earn back 10 or 20 times that amount in no time?" You are going to hear the words "we don't have any revenue yet, but we're close" and "about to cross over" more times than you can count.

If you're wondering how often this kind of offer comes to something positive for the former business owner, how often they get into some previously unknown business just a quarter before profits start rolling in, how often they make a next-level fortune on an approach from a stranger, the answer is almost never.

As a general rule, if you don't know the industry, the company, and especially the people in question, you shouldn't waste your time entertaining the idea of investing.

PUT EXPERT ADVICE IN PERSPECTIVE

Professional consultants often play a part before and after the sale. A good CPA and tax attorney are great assets, but you must also be independent-minded. I have witnessed firsthand a number of business owners who are somehow working for their CPA or attorney instead of the other way around. Most of these people know less than you do about investing, because they don't have to look at the big picture. They have never met payroll at large companies, leveraged assets, or invested large amounts of capital to get a return. I can't count how often I've heard these words: "My advisor is against it," when the advisor in question is someone with a very narrow scope of view and function. Maybe they do the taxes, or maybe they draw up the contracts. Often they've offered good advice in some other area. Whatever the case, I strongly suggest you ask the question, *Why does this person advise against?* Be certain that a lack of knowledge or deep understanding isn't a factor. By all means, listen to your advisors, but remember to keep those recommendations in perspective.

KEEP YOUR OWN COUNSEL

One piece of advice that will serve former business owners during the turbulent time after the sale is to stay in tune with both heart and mind. You built a successful, profitable business worth millions. You created jobs and products and value. You likely know how to read people, and you have strong business instincts that have helped bring you this far. Whether you're dealing with family members, friends, accountants, lawyers, or strangers offering you the "opportunity of a lifetime," don't lose sight of the shrewdness, thoughtfulness, and sometimes the gut sense that got you this far. Right after you sell your business is the worst possible time to start questioning your competence or putting too much stock in the voices of strangers.

If you respect someone, hear them out. Mentors and experts can be a tremendous help when it comes to details, but your job is the big picture. Give yourself credit for being able to better recognize what is right for you than anyone else.

I say this as someone who long ago discovered that business owners are some of my own best consultants. When I need advice or business help, they are my greatest assets. They have seen almost every situation—from being broke to taking incredible chances to stay afloat. Most business owners have excellent people skills as well as compassion. They've had to be both tough and tender at times. And their knowledge can be encyclopedic.

As you navigate this critical time, remember your own great traits. Mix them with a dose of caution while you adjust to your new circumstances. Greed, indiscretion, and high risk are the cardinal sins of investing and can quickly destroy a fortune that took decades to build, but as long as you carefully screen your consultants and analyze each major recommendation with a cool head, you'll be fine.

CHAPTER 10

$15 Million and Broke

M ost people would wonder how in the world a business owner could sell out and end up losing $15 million, $25 million—or unbelievably $100 million. It sounds unlikely. Over the last 30-plus years, however, I have seen a number of former business owners do just that. In fact, I never have a year go by that I don't see somebody flush it all. They simply don't have sufficient respect for how much money they have—or how hard it would be to replace.

Owners who lose their post-sale money usually follow one of three patterns:

PATTERN #1: THE OWNER WHO DOESN'T RECOGNIZE DIMINISHING WEALTH

This owner sells the company, for example, at $15 million, thinking anyone can live indefinitely on that. He should be right, but then he makes a series of decisions that seem, at the time, like logical indulgences. Taxes after the sale come to $2.5 million, leaving $12.5 million in principal. The business owner then buys a beach house with all the trimmings for $2 million and remodels a current home for $1 million. Now the balance is $9.5 million. Each of the children hit up Mom and Dad for $500,000 of the wealth. The former owner, now a newly minted entrepreneur with deep pockets, invests $1.5 million in a totally unfamiliar business. That brings the base balance to $7 million. The former business owner is needing to draw $500,000 per year out of principal to meet new sky-high living expenses. By the end of the third year, the total has shrunk to $5.5 million in liquid investments. It may be far less if the owner has also been jumping on "hot" stock tips and losing in the markets. The business in which he reinvested still isn't producing. If this individual doesn't get an income stream, the remaining liquid capital will be gone in just a few years.

Of particular note here is the difference in first-, second-, and third-generation wealth. Malcolm Forbes used to say, "Shirtsleeves to shirtsleeves in three generations." The first generation builds it, the second generation sells it, and the third generation spends it. I am just as impressed with a second-generation business builder who realizes what mental hurdles must be overcome to sell a business and then to maintain prosperity as I am with the first-generation entrepreneur. The group wherein most of the risk lies is the third generation. These individuals did not build, operate, or sell the business; therefore, they tend to underappreciate what it takes to make money and keep it.

The other group I see going through this process again and again are those who made their money in a hurry. There's a fundamental difference in the financial mindset of someone who worked for decades to amass an amount of wealth and someone who came into it over just a few years (or faster). At Oxbow, we see this sometimes with lottery winners, with celebrities in the entertainment and sports worlds, and with individuals who sold tech companies that were little more than a great idea for tens of millions. They operate under the assumption that lightning will strike for them again, that there's always another big payday right around the corner. Unfortunately, that's rarely the case.

PATTERN #2: THE OWNER WHOSE FORTUNE IS TIED TO THE COMPANY

In this case, the new owners of the company, whether public or private, somehow convinced the owner to put a lot of money back into the business (or to leave it there) as part of the deal. In theory, this makes sense. The selling owner built the company, and it's likely been profitable if it's the subject of a big sale. In practice, though, this is something that often backfires. No longer in a controlling position, the former owner may have to sit back and watch not only as the new owners make inadvisable decisions about the direction of the company but also as their personal wealth is diminished by those choices.

The crux of the problem here comes down to the buying entity using the seller as a bank. They'll tell you they'll pay $60 million for your company, but ask you to put back $20 million so you're invested in their future success. In reality, they're just avoiding paying you in full, and they're tying your financial fate to what they do next with your former company. Think about it this way: Why would you trade the ability to control your company for an illiquid asset tied to a company you cannot steer? It's the worst of all worlds, because you own it, you don't control it, and you likely can't sell it.

The best way to avoid this situation is to not tie up your own capital with the company's in the deal in the first place. After the sale, the next best thing is to look for your earliest and easiest path to fully extricating your money.

PATTERN #3: THE OWNER WHO *MUST* BE IN BUSINESS, EVEN THE WRONG ONE

The third type of owner who sells is the has-to-be-in-business person (or more accurately, the has-to-be-the-boss person). After selling, this individual is so lost and disoriented that jumping directly into another business dominates their thoughts. Over the years, I have observed far too many of these people who seem to decide that being in *any* business is more important than being in the *right* business.

An example is Wayne, who exchanged his portion of a partnership for stock in a publicly owned corporation. Although he was the number three partner and successful primarily because of the other two owners, he nevertheless received a substantial after-tax dollar amount for the sale of his shares. He immediately bought another business, and over the next four years, I sadly bore witness to his total financial demise. My last correspondence with him was regarding an IRS tax-lien letter. This is someone whose need to be the big man outweighed every other practical and reasonable concern.

My principal theory about these types of people is that their post-sale mindset is the crucial variable. Interestingly, most seemed to be relaxed, even after losing it all. In my opinion, these individuals never were comfortable with a lot of money. They had a hard time seeing themselves as "rich." Many had spent so much time with their backs to the wall struggling with debt, as opposed to the fleeting fling with fortune, that "struggle" was a natural state of affairs for them. Their adrenaline flowed most strongly when the battle was the toughest. They seemed to have the feeling that nothing, even life itself, should be easy—and they had surprisingly philosophical outlooks on both winning and losing.

There's a great book about the surprising psychological changes that come with wealth called *Strangers in Paradise*, by James Grubman, PhD. In it, the author compares the newly wealthy to people who are immigrating to a new land from their old home. In the new land, they have money and all the freedom that comes with it, but they also have the burdens that come from moving to a new place, one where life is different from what they knew before. Some people find themselves out of their element in that new place, and I believe a percentage make the decision, consciously or unconsciously, to try to return to their old, comfortable "home" and relationships as they were before. Many old friendships are permanently altered, though—regardless of whether the individual is able to get comfortable with the wealth or not.

I want to be clear here because this chapter pulls back the curtain on some poor choices and negative outcomes: Many business owners establish or participate in a second or third business and do even better than in the first—or at least operate profitable enterprises. Some sellers who lose all their money come back and do better the second time. In fact, most of them manage just fine. In my observation, though, between 5% and 10% end up losing most of their wealth. That small percentage can teach us all a lot about what not to do with new liquidity.

OXBOW NOTE

In my book $20 Million and Broke, *I outline the reasons wealth loss is so common in detail and with real-life examples. If you'd like a complimentary copy of this book or any of my other titles, contact us at OxbowAdvisors.com.*

CHAPTER 11

Security Is in the Mind

Everybody wants to feel financially secure. As a business owner, that's what you were building toward. After selling, you probably thought your security had come to stay in the form of cash in the bank and the absence of debt. Life ahead would be easy because all problems had disappeared. But does that really happen?

Only in the movies.

I have two stories I'd like to share with you regarding security.

FEELING SECURE WITH $1.3 MILLION

Gary was the owner of a Southeastern service enterprise that he sold to a public company. He received about $2 million of value in stock and wisely sold enough to pay off all debt and put $500,000 in the bank. He and his wife were quite frugal and wanted to be debt-free with about $800,000 of stock before paying the tax obligation. So they lived on the income from CDs and watched for potential business deals.

I visited with them over a period of several years in order to discuss their financial situation. Gary and his wife felt very secure. Seeing them always reminded me that money cannot buy that feeling. He said he was perfectly happy playing golf in Florida, then coming home to Tennessee just to enjoy life. The couple wasn't worried about tomorrow. Living for today was enjoyable and fulfilling for both of them. In the winter they would go to their hunting cabin and stay for a few months. They lived on very little, but they were psychologically and emotionally secure.

The recession of 2001 and 2002 brought a big real estate bust to the Southeast. Gary and his wife practically stole a house at 50% of value near a golf course. Biding their time was paying off, though they would've gladly stayed in the old house had a new opportunity not arrived. They also had a chance to buy a glass company, where both of them began working. This started providing more income, and then a new investment opportunity arrived. For $150,000 they were able to purchase 50% ownership of a car dealership.

Each time I visited this couple, they displayed the same peaceful security, even serenity. They thought $1.3 million was plenty to have, even if nothing worked out with their new ventures. They would be fine. It was abundantly clear to me that their sense of security came from within.

FEELING INSECURE WITH $30 MILLION

My next story involves Tom, who sold a service company in Texas and received about $30 million in cash. He had personally experienced excellent growth in the company he sold and expected to match those results in his own investing. Tom couldn't wait to start buying more companies and attaining an even larger net worth. He was convinced that $30 million was not enough. He invested heavily in two banks, as well as in three or four other businesses. This was at a time when most businesses in the Southwest were performing well.

Our discussions of investing in other areas were always too mundane for him. He couldn't see getting to his larger goals by investing in a traditional manner. He was impatient with any slow process.

Over the next six years, Tom managed to lose all the money in the banks and most of the money in the businesses. The Southwestern economy was bludgeoned for a period of time, and so was his net worth.

I encountered Tom again years later when he was trying to get a small company started with a new patent. His net worth was no more than $1 million liquid. To the best of my knowledge, he never found security.

In the years since these two stories played out, I've seen this relativity when it comes to security time and again. I've seen people with $150 million who can barely sleep at night for worry about their net worth, and I've seen people who have just enough wealth to assure they'll never actually go hungry count their blessings and rest easy every day. The only way this all makes sense is when we agree on the bedrock truth that "security" is a state of mind. It is not defined by any universal number. The answer to the age-old question of *What is enough?* is different for each of us. Everyone needs to be sensible with assets through saving and investing, but that feeling that everything is going to be okay? That only comes from making peace with yourself.

Some people are fine with their sense of security resting on shifting sands, but for those who want to feel better, to learn how to be comfortable with what they have instead of driven to worry about it day and night, these are the lessons I've learned from investors who are truly comfortable with the wealth they have:

- *Learn to be still.* Business owners are in the habit of being busy, busy, busy from the time they open their eyes in the morning until they close them at night. In the midst of their long, hectic days, they rarely have time to be quiet and contemplate. You don't meet a lot of business owners who meditate. That's a shame, because putting all the mental churning on pause, for even a few minutes every day, allows the mind to reset and focus.

If you're in the process of walking away from a chaotic, demanding business life, find a way to be still every day and see what your mind brings you. Among the first realizations is often the fact that you don't have to get your energy from adrenaline. You have powerful inner energy that's waiting to be tapped, but you've got to give it a chance to replace that urgency you're used to after running a company.

- *Easy on the vices.* When a person who's spent 30 or 40 years working nonstop finally gets a little free time, sometimes things go south pretty quick. After spending decades thinking about the same things every day and then having it all come to a grinding halt, some former business owners don't know much of relaxation outside of the idea of occasional vacations and cocktails. So that's what they do. Flush with cash, they book a villa in the Caribbean and take up gambling or start happy hour a little earlier every day. It's an easy path to get on and sometimes a hard one to step off. It's also one that feeds insecurity, so while you're learning to feel comfortable and secure with your newfound wealth, be sure to keep your favorite indulgences from growing into problems during the process.

The opposite of this kind of uber-vacation mentality is one that embraces a different kind of full life. Ask yourself what's truly good in your life, what makes you feel clear and happy and at peace. Maybe it's your grandkids. Maybe it's doing charitable work. Maybe it's taking a trip somewhere beautiful with your spouse or finally having time to golf or hike or coach a sports team. Whatever it is, let it help you fill some of the empty spaces of your new post-business life.

- *Do the math.* Among the investors I've worked with, there have been many individuals who are in their 70s, 80s, or older who have $30 million or more in the bank, withdraw far less than that wealth generates each year, and still lose sleep about money. These are people who should feel entirely secure who have internalized abstract and unrealistic fears. If this sounds familiar, sit down with your investment advisor and your calculator and work it out. What does your income generate every year, and what do you spend? What would happen if you tapped into your principal? I recently had a client who was so worried about this I laid it out in terms of lifespan. If she never made another penny and withdrew $1 million a year (far more than she was actually spending), she'd be flush until she reached 112 years old. What I wanted for her was for money to be a source of comfort in her life, not a source of anxiety. There was simply no need for her to worry about it.

There are plenty of investors out there who ought to be worried about whether their wealth will last. If you've sold your company and are making prudent choices, there's no reason for you to be among them.

CHAPTER 12

Happiness and Purpose: Two Sides of the Same Coin

A quote that's been attributed to everyone from Immanuel Kant to Elvis Presley goes like this: *Happiness is having something to do, someone to love, and something to hope for.*

For individuals who've achieved the ultimate financial success, the adage can be a little problematic. Many business owners get so embroiled in building and running their companies that professional success becomes all things to them. When they reach the point where somebody offers tens of millions (or hundreds of millions) for the business, many of them expect that happiness will arrive automatically with the money.

That expectation can lead to disappointment. In reality, happiness often takes a hit in the aftermath of the sale of a business. A person's "something to do" changes dramatically. Overnight, the seller goes from having a company to run and employees to manage and customers to answer—all the way over to days that have no plans past breakfast.

For better or worse, relationships shift too. Firstly, the business owner loses the constant interaction—and often the affection—that comes from employees and colleagues. Second, friendships can be strained—sometimes temporarily and sometimes forever—when one party experiences a total change of financial circumstances. And while many couples and families stay close regardless of their fortunes, there are always a few individuals who, faced with the prospect of total financial independence, prefer to go their separate ways.

Having something to hope for is also deeply impacted by the sale of the company. People almost universally hope for financial security. When they achieve it, that success leaves a big empty space. The lucky ones already have higher and better hopes in place, but not everyone does.

In many ways, figuring out your new purpose is key to happiness after the sale.

A TALE OF TWO BUSINESSMEN

Some people get this really right, and others make themselves miserable. One of the most satisfied former business owners I know found his purpose—and his happiness—in family. Roger sold two different companies and ended up with a significant fortune. Before, during, and after the sale, he was always content. He was grateful for the freedom his wealth afforded but not caught up in the ego and power that so often come hand in hand with money. He had great relationships with family and friends, and even as those shifted, he stayed centered and happy.

Fred's situation played out in another way. He was a client in the Southeast who sold his company for a large sum. His children were grown, he had met all his professional goals, and he had enough money to do anything he wanted. It should have been a recipe for happiness, but it wasn't. Instead of finding new purpose in something positive, Fred poured his heart and soul into a long, contentious divorce. He turned his focus to controlling his soon-to-be ex-wife, spending years in revenge mode and millions of dollars along the way.

If you'd asked (and I did) what it would take for him to be happy, Fred would have told you it was seeing his ex lose everything. The negativity of his purpose kept him from finding any real contentment for the rest of his life.

Roger's and Fred's stories are extreme examples: a man who

gravitated toward happiness and one who drifted toward misery. You could argue that the difference in their fates was based in their circumstances, but happiness, like security, is largely defined by the individual. Either one of these people could have gone the other way—choosing to be content or to be dissatisfied and angry. We all know someone in our lives who can't find happiness no matter what they have—and someone who manages to be happy even in the face of illness, family struggles, or personal tragedy.

TRANSITION TIMES

Many business owners only realize after the sale that much of their happiness came from running the company. They were fulfilled when they were managing operations, doing deals, interacting with employees, and functioning in an environment where they were frequently the most knowledgeable person in the room. Many times I've had poignant meetings with business owners who are on the other side of a sale and looking back at those days, longing for the full schedule and sense of accomplishment they provided.

A number of owners have told me they regret having sold—and some have gotten back into business and found happiness there again. For many, though, this period of emptiness and uncertainty about whether they did the right thing is temporary—a time of adjustment as they find new purpose and new sources of good feelings.

The people who navigate this change best are the ones who stay active on multiple fronts. They continue to cultivate relationships, for example—with family, with friends, and with business associates. They know that even though those relationships are shifting, they're still worthwhile.

Many are engaged in something charity- or community-oriented. They may be on the board of a charity or head a committee in their church. They may help oversee scholarship selections or support a project close to their heart. And a lot of these people are doing a tremendous amount of good because they're offering a lifetime of learning and business acumen to organizations that can greatly benefit from their participation.

Many are also perked up for new professional and investment opportunities, taking their time and putting themselves into the frame of mind of learning something new.

AN APT COMPARISON

One comparison that usually hits home for former business owners is the one to retired professional athletes. There's a stark before and after to the two phases of life. Out of the action, athletes miss the bright lights, the adrenaline-filled game days, and the appreciation of the crowd. Many even miss the routines of training. Former business owners miss many of the same things: the routines, the action, the adrenaline, and the appreciation and admiration.

But there are things these groups don't miss. Things like not having time for even simple pleasures with their families. Not having room in the schedule to simply relax. Not being able to afford the luxury of a hobby, or an amateur sport, or choosing to explore a new interest without constant pressure to hurry up and move on.

My best advice for anyone entering this phase after the sale is to devote some energy to the soul searching you likely haven't had time for in ages. Step away from the business, go off somewhere, and ask some big questions, about your higher purpose, about your ability to be a positive influence for others, and about where and when you feel happy and useful. Consider without pressure, remembering that you have both time and freedom. As you find new purpose, you will also find new happiness.

CHAPTER 13

Market Declines and Foreseeable Disasters

In recent years we've had three periods where investor greed overtook rational thinking to an extreme extent: leading up to the tech bust of 2000, the great financial crisis of 2007–09, and, as I write these pages in early 2022, Covid-era investor hype. This is a time when stocks, bonds, cryptocurrencies and NFTs, special-purpose acquisitions, art, real estate of all kinds, and private companies of all stripes are selling for outrageous prices. There isn't even a whiff of caution in the air. Like the previous frenzies, it is defined by an overzealous drive to get in on the climb at any price.

It seems very few people have any memory of the last excruciating crash (or the ones before it). That great financial crisis took a similar path to Covid-era investing, with a great deal of loose money in the economy getting over into real estate. Suddenly every home and condo was getting bid up—and very few were bought with substantial money down. What happened in 2007–09, however, pales in comparison to the money grab in progress in 2022—a frenzy that's been emboldened by the Federal Reserve's steady juicing of the economy. The Fed may have done its greatest disservice ever to the country during this period.

Why is this particularly relevant for business owners who have sold or are considering selling? In part it's about the money they're receiving. I've told many business owners who've sold their companies during the Covid period, "You picked the best time ever to sell your company. It may never be worth this much again." Unfortunately, there's a corollary to that. Those who turned right around and invested that money likely did so at the worst time ever.

My reminder to owners who know full well they got more than their companies were worth when they sold (and most of them do know) is that they've got a built-in financial cushion thanks to that overvaluation. With that in mind, they can afford to sit on the cash for a while. It may not take an investment genius to recognize when an economic cycle is nearing the top, but it certainly takes a steady hand and self-control to stay on the sidelines while the period of euphoria plays out.

A LITTLE KNOWLEDGE IS A LITTLE DANGEROUS

One thing I consistently observe during boom-and-bust eras is the ignorance of the investment world among many business entrepreneurs. A basic lack of experience in the field is often compounded with a dash of arrogance—forgetting that a little knowledge is a dangerous thing. Many have mistaken their entrepreneurial acumen for investment wisdom, thinking their business sense was the sole linchpin of their wealth. In Oxbow's history we have witnessed many benighted souls who didn't realize that financial luck and rare opportunities come calling only once or twice in a lifetime. While there's no question hard work and intelligence play key roles in entrepreneurial success, there's also no question that things like timing and simple good fortune factor in as well. So many young people in particular fail to recognize the hand-of-fate factor. They are quick to blow opportunities for lifelong financial security with the rationale "I know this stock will come back . . . It's just a matter of patience and a little time."

Too often, former business owners who spent decades making prudent financial decisions get caught up in a hot market and go chasing. They end up buying into things they'd never have touched as independent business operators. They learn just enough about investing to feel confident in their decisions but not enough to understand the larger and sometimes more subtle forces at work in an economy.

Time and again I've seen these investors double down and stay stubbornly entrenched in questionable positions—especially in a rising market. It can be hard to resist the temptation of seemingly easy money, choosing to diversify when one or two segments of the economy are screaming up and up. At the turn of the century, even my own partners and I, with more than 20 years' experience then, had to ask ourselves if we could be out of step with the times. We decided that was not the case, but we were continually confronting the outrageous prices internet companies were paying for high-tech start-ups with almost no tangible assets. Their actions cracked a whip over the entire market, pushing values to new heights. Clients told us the dot-com boom was expanding beyond any range or scope that we could realize or even imagine. This early phase, they said, was a mere drop in the profit bucket, which would overflow in the not-too-distant future. Their comments seemed to imply a warranty in general about internet market prices. In fact, most of these clients would append a gratuitous dismissal to us, which said in effect: "Why do we need you when we've created all this wealth on our own?"

One of our clients, located in California, underscored this reaction. Susan received a huge fortune after the sale of a business she founded, one that had been in operation a relatively short period of time. During our contact, she told us we were like her father, as we also believed in "obsolete" criteria about market values (things like earnings-per-share record, book value, price-earnings multiples, dividend histories, and many others). The insinuation was clear: We were investment-advisor dinosaurs.

Almost exactly two years later, along with millions of other investors who'd grabbed on to the dot-com comet with everything they had, Susan had a front-row seat for one of the biggest market declines since the post-Depression era. Her tech-heavy portfolio dropped like a stone, wiping out more than 90% of her assets. The young lady who'd told us, verbatim, "You just don't get it," was back at square one.

THE GREED FACTOR

We all know that on some level greed is simply part of the human experience. At one time or another, we're all guilty of it. How much more damage can it do, though, when it's allowed to run rampant—especially in someone who otherwise has a lock on a lifetime of financial security and the personal freedom that affords? In the early months of the new millennium, in the run-up to the great financial crisis, and again in the early 2020s, investors who already had everything chose to show an utter disdain for historical investment data and plain common sense.

During each of these economic cycles, I was asked by clients who were already financially secure to give them my best investment advice. For many, especially those who were young and "playing" the markets with money they could otherwise count on to support them for the rest of their lives, my recommendation was to sell. Sadly, this wasn't what most of them wanted to hear, and they were doomed to hit the wall at some point and finally learn how hard it is not only to acquire substantial net worth but also to retain it. Many ultimately found themselves looking back and asking, *What was I thinking? How could I have botched my golden opportunity for financial security?*

CHAPTER 14

Real Estate: It Can't Go Down (Can It?)

R eal estate has always been a staple in the investment portfolios of business owners after selling. Property investments come in many different packages, but most former owners like them because their businesses owned real estate, making them de facto owner-operators. An owner may have bought a building for offices or purchased industrial space. In each case, they became their own tenant—a highly palatable arrangement for the lending bank. When these owners ultimately sold, as part of the sale of the company or outside of it, they did well. That's a great situation, but it leads many former business owners to come into the investment stage of their lives with the idea that all real estate will have similar outcomes.

This isn't always the case. Sure, most business owners who sold their companies from 1990 to 2008 caught the real estate market right and came out ahead. Declining interest rates coupled with ideal supply/demand demographics made for great returns.

However, when buying and selling real estate *is* the business (vs. is one small aspect of the business), that changes everything. Things like maintenance and tenant management take up a disproportionate amount of time. And despite the sometimes fickle nature of the market, those who rely on real estate investments for income require steady returns.

Real estate has always been a natural fit for former business owners looking to invest—and for good reason. They like that they're looking at hard assets: a parking lot and a building. An investor may look at a facility that has a pharmacy, for example, and trust they can buy the building and lease it back to the tenant for 10 or 20 years at a 7% return. The investment may play out exactly as expected, but savvy investors will remember times when real estate got real sticky. Any property owner who's been hit by the crushing blows to retail in the age of internet shopping can attest to this.

NEVER-ENDING PRICE CLIMB

One of the trends we at Oxbow noticed starting in 2000–02 was a seemingly never-ending price rise in real estate. Practically everyone who sold a business would purchase at least some property with the proceeds. The 15-year span between 1990 and 2005 was the perfect setup for the "baby boomer" generation.

Bernard was a former owner of an equipment company that sold out in the late 1990s. He and his wife called me one day in 2005 to discuss a waterfront lot they had purchased for $600,000. They were going to build on the land, but prices had gone so high they were offered almost $5 million just for the land. They asked my advice, and the answer came easily: Sell the property and pocket the proceeds. The real estate craze was so big, however, that they decided to keep the property and started building. A few terrible storms and a lousy builder later, the profits were gone. They ended up taking millions less and an overall loss on the deal.

When the economy collapsed in 2008, we saw real estate at all levels decline dramatically. In the aftermath, it began an excruciatingly slow climb—right up until the price explosion in the Covid era. The pattern of frenzied buying over all reasonable estimates of value is once again a giant red flag that should be warning potential investors that it's time to sit tight and wait.

INVESTING IN THOSE WITH NOTHING TO LOSE

Another big mistake Oxbow frequently sees former business owners make is investing in projects with developers who don't have anything to lose in the deal. Alvin was a client for more than

15 years, and during that time, we continually liquidated investments to meet his partners' needs to build shopping centers. He could have produced a lifetime of income, but instead he chose to go with illiquid real estate. Time and again he got in deep with a developer, until the bulk of his cash reserves were up in smoke.

This scenario is all too common. A developer with modest net worth has little to lose if a deal doesn't work. From that position, it makes perfect sense to swing for the fences. Worst case, they'll eventually need a new big idea and somebody new with money to get behind it. The initial investor's money, however, will be long gone.

Trusting the assets from selling your company to someone else is risky business. If you choose to invest in speculative real estate, then control the deal yourself, just like you did when you owned the company.

REAL ESTATE UNDER PRESSURE

Starting about 2007, the trend of online shopping emerged and began impacting commercial real estate across the country. A shift toward working at home and a growing gig economy have equally undermined the premiums that were once expected for offices and business spaces. At this writing, residential real estate has been on a long climb. It remains to be seen what will happen when the baby boomer generation, with many so far content to age in place at home, makes the move to selling. Larger than the generations before and after them, they have the potential to create a seismic impact on property markets—especially as the generations below Gen X are so far not nearly as intent on owning real estate as the ones that preceded them.

Business owners in the future will need to be wary of getting trapped in illiquidity. They can't count on price jumps to continue to bail them out regardless of cash flow. Needing to produce cash flow but being locked into a maintenance-heavy, tax-eating investment with little or no net free cash flow can create a scenario where hard choices must be made. The need to have a disciplined, measured, and diligent approach to investing in real estate is never more important than when investing proceeds from a sale.

FROM RED HOT TO ICE COLD

Art was a client who sold a business in Colorado in 2002. Having watched stocks get hammered soon after the turn of the century, he made the decision to develop land and real estate. The real estate markets were red hot in 2005, and he called and liquidated almost everything. The proceeds went entirely into real estate. By 2009 he had lost virtually all of it, with no cash flow and major cash calls.

Situations like these do not need to happen when former owners step back and look at the larger landscape. Given the same circumstances when they ran a business, this would not have happened. After selling, business owners need to be careful about succumbing to rose-colored-glasses syndrome. Everything looks possible, and they tend to grossly overassess their ability to invest.

The attractiveness of real estate will always be there, but so will the need to assess correctly. Keep these significant points in mind:

- If your business investment in real estate cash flows is not more than 20% over a high-grade bond portfolio, be careful.

- If you're going to be completely illiquid and depend solely on a sale or takeout, be careful.

- If you intend to have a partner, be careful. Very few business owners would ever have had a partner in their companies, so why do it so easily in real estate?

Real property has a place as a cornerstone of the investment process, but it should always be undertaken with a careful assessment of potential cash flow and the challenges of an exit strategy.

CHAPTER 15

The Wall Street Shuffle

A fter selling their companies, most business owners have proceeds that must eventually be reinvested. That reinvestment can come in the form of real estate, commodities, businesses, or financial investments. In my decades of investment management, working alongside others in my firm with 45-plus years of experience, one conclusion stands out: The greatest risk to financial health and well-being comes directly from Wall Street and the firms it controls. The greed that has spewed forth from these investment marketing firms leaves no other industry a close second, and it reverberates from the top on down.

In our lengthy history of watching people sell businesses, we at Oxbow have continually been amazed at the lack of skill, integrity, and respect for large sums of money most of these Wall Street firms exhibit. In this chapter it is my hope that you will get some insight into why this happens and what to look for. Several misconceptions come to mind:

MISCONCEPTION #1: THIS ONE LOOKS GREAT

Firms have a tendency to recommend exposure: potentially volatile and, most importantly, illiquid investments. This is because they normally get paid more to offer these items. How many times does the former business owner get offered a really conservative investment at a really low cost? Many of the incentives for Wall Street are based on volume and quantity instead of quality. The former business owner would never have invested company funds in anything inherently risky, but many readily do so with their newfound wealth.

MISCONCEPTION #2: I'M DEALING WITH AN EXPERT

Former business owners have experience in their industries, and they often take for granted that the people they are dealing with in the investment world are the decision makers. They shouldn't be so sure. When you're working with Wall Street firms, it's all too easy to find yourself being "managed" by someone who is the third or fourth removed from the true money manager. *Financial advisor, financial planner, account executive,* and *investment team* are all names for people who do not actually make investment decisions. There's a huge difference between dealing with an up-and-coming person who is essentially in sales for Wall Street and dealing with a seasoned investment expert. If you're not sure who you're shaking hands with in any given firm, ask the question: *Are you the person directly making the decisions about what's happening with my money? If not, who, exactly, is making those calls?*

Keep in mind that a shockingly high percentage of so-called financial advisors have little or no personal net worth. Many are simply working their way up the ladder, playing their small role in a conglomerate where they remain far removed from decisions with consequences. At Oxbow, we directly manage our investments.

Regardless of who you choose to help guide your investment decisions, be sure you know how the org chart works and who is actually buying and selling with your funds.

MISCONCEPTION #3: LAST YEAR'S WINE IS BEST

People in the money management business have a pronounced tendency to offer the former business owner investments that have performed well over the most recent three- to five-year period. Unfortunately, this is usually the worst time to begin investing in these areas. Studies have shown that the worst-performing assets over the last five years in many cases become the best for the years ahead. Too often, Wall Street types focus on looking backward rather than looking forward.

MISCONCEPTION #4: FORMER BUSINESS OWNERS ARE KNOWLEDGEABLE INVESTORS

When it comes to the actual analysis of individual investments, owners typically have little skill and little experience. Unfortunately, many of the people offering these investments—and advice about them—have limited skill as well. The disadvantage comes from an almost total inability of the former business owner—new to this world—to distinguish the good advice from the bad. New to the investment field, former owners are then relegated to accepting what they are being told.

The fact is, large liquid wealth is hard to come by, and so people who have it need to dig a little deeper and make more careful choices. Just because you like someone doesn't mean that person is a competent advisor. Just because someone says something is a tremendous opportunity doesn't mean it is. Just because a financial consultant or team has a Wall Street name doesn't mean they have a legitimate commitment to preserving your wealth or to making decisions consistent with your long-term priorities.

It is also far too easy to get caught up in the hype of some company that catches your eye. You may be familiar with a company in principle, but that's often worse than coming at it as an unknown entity. You may make a purchase based on an image or a story in the news. If you took an interest in Peloton, for example, in January of 2021, you'd have been assessing a hot item. That month, the company's stock sat at 170, and beginner's logic might have concluded it could only go up. You might have skipped the tremendous amount of analysis a seasoned advisor would have put into the investment. You might have failed to consider the management team, the overall trends in the industry, and the competitors storming the market. Twelve months later, when the stock was down to 35, you would have thought the drop was inexplicable, but it was not.

An investor who leads with, simply, *I like Company X* is making critical financial decisions based on hunches and personal affinities and mystery factors like what's put in front of them by a Wall Street advisor or even social media ads. No business owner I've known chose vendors, partners, or clients this way when they were running the company, but far too many of them do it once they've cashed out the business and moved on to their age of investment.

At a minimum, everyone who's sold a business should consider whether they'd ever have dreamed of investing in that public company when it was private.

Many former business owners know just enough Wall Street jargon and "investment speak" to sound knowledgeable. Following are just three pitfalls of which they should be aware:

Pitfall #1: Too many high-risk/ high-reward investments

Wall Street loves to offer what former business owners thrive on the most: the sweet sound of high returns and above-average profits. Remember the sirens' song of Greek mythology, almost causing Odysseus to crash his craft on the rocks? After all, high returns and strong profits are what business owners spend their entire lives trying to find. They invariably underestimate the level of risk in these areas. Worst of all, the former business owners assume most of the risk. Witness the proliferation of hedge funds, popping up like mushrooms on a damp night, over the last 10–20 years.

Pitfall #2: Overallocation to the investment class

Asset allocation has long been a Wall Street buzz phrase, and it has taken the concept to extremes by allocating to almost every single area. When investors allocate sums of money to an inordinate amount of areas, they become so diversified that no one wins. Except—you guessed it—Wall Street. Being completely diversified means the financial advisors don't have to make tough choices about where to put emphasis. If Warren Buffett, Charlie Munger, and John Templeton were totally diversified, they would not be nearly as wealthy as they are today. Most former business owners don't have the knowledge or experience to know the correct mix. Diversification in and of itself is not always correct.

Walter was a great guy who sold a large contracting firm in the Southeast. It was just prior to the 1987 meltdown in the stock market. He felt a powerful pull to follow a large Wall Street firm's advice, so he allocated most of his financial resources to an array of stock market styles fronting as diversification. When I told him that he should have more liquidity at one point than in the previous five years, he passed. As has occurred so many times over the years, his call came after the stock market dropped 30% on October 19, 1987. Most business owners have an intuitive sense about when to pull things in a bit when it comes to their own company. They would be well served to seek out people in the investment management field who share that same respect for appropriate caution.

Pitfall #3: Not protecting the base

When a business is sold, the former owner will need to have some base capital that produces the needed monthly cash flow. This is the part of the assets that have to be allocated toward producing income. Base capital and investing capital are entirely different. Base capital is the machine that produces income. Investing capital is everything else. Former owners of businesses almost always underestimate the amount of cash flow needed, because they've become accustomed to having cash flow at their fingertips from the business.

Wall Street has an almost compulsive tendency to overemphasize growth and underemphasize cash flow. In practice, this is in reverse of what it should be. After a business is sold, base capital will have to produce for a long time. The worst thing to do is not prepare for enough cash flow, then let the stock market decline and draw down at a critical time. Be sure to hold fast when it comes to the amount of base capital that is used for cash flow. Do not let Wall Street lead you astray on this.

In addition, be very clear about just how much of your total capital needs to be totally protected. After these two areas are covered, you can move on to investment capital that is above and beyond your base.

Lastly, I have four tips for former business owners as they figure out their relationship with Wall Street.

TIP #1: WATCH FOR CURVE BALLS

One of the most misunderstood areas of investing for the former owner involves being able to watch for curves being thrown relative to investing. Most former business owners don't have a good frame of reference when it comes to some of the spin that Wall Street puts on its pitches.

Connie approached me some years ago about a Florida money manager who showed fantastic results in a hypothetical illustration of investment history. I pointed out to her that the results were skewed because the firm made all of its returns over a two-year period in one stock (Apple). My question to her was: "What would happen if you didn't catch those two years? Then you'd be below average."

Hypothetical returns can be very misleading, and it takes a skilled eye to extricate the details. As an individual who just sold a business, you need to concentrate first on protecting the principal, second on producing a cash-flow stream, and third on getting upside. Wall Street can run circles around a person with what-ifs and hypotheticals.

TIP #2: KEEP ASKING, "RELATIVE TO WHAT?"

One of Wall Street's most famous gigs is discussing returns in terms of relative performance to some index. It goes something like this: "Mr. Former Owner, you should be happy that your portfolio is only down –18%. The overall stock market is down –23%, so you have done much better on a relative basis." This is tantamount to a former business owner saying, "Your company lost a lot of money, but your competitors did worse." How many business owners feel good about losing money? Not many I know of. Beware of the Wall Street relative-return game. It can cost you a lot of precious investment capital.

TIP #3: LOOK AT THE TERM

Another Wall Street stratagem is to show results over the extreme long term. It isn't unusual for Wall Street to show 15-, 20-, or even 40-year results. Most of these results will mean very little in the future. Most business owners plan about a year in advance. Trying to consider an extremely long-term time frame doesn't fit with their normal style of analysis. Business owners seldom think about 20 years in the future. They spend most of their time in one- to three-year time frames of plans and goals. Wall Street people would love to have everyone look at long-term time frames in order that the short term doesn't get addressed.

TIP #4: USE BUSINESS COMMON SENSE

Business owners are some of the best decision makers in the world. Wall Street has some of the worst decision makers in the world. Former business owners should trust their instincts on what is best for them. Do not fall prey to the ongoing litany of information that doesn't apply to your situation. Remember to watch out for your own asset protection in every case. Wall Street will get more customers, but more than likely you will not sell another company—so stay conservative.

OXBOW NOTE

First-generation wealth earners need to constantly guard against schemes designed to separate them from their wealth. These tests of your judgment don't always come in the form of shady characters with questionable reputations. Many show up polished, with the sheen of

Wall Street on them. Just remember the caveat about buyer beware. If you'd like a free copy of Oxbow's analysis of the scams designed to separate you from your money, Wall Street Lies: 5 Myths to Keep Your Cash in Their Game, *contact us at OxbowAdvisors.com.*

CHAPTER 16

Investment Planning for the Future

After selling a company, the business owner will have new semiliquid assets. They usually take the form of cash, stock, notes, or convertible bonds. In any case, the former owner has investment-planning work to do. Over the years, I have met many recent sellers who failed to generate a three- to five-year plan. In almost all cases, little consideration was given to the need for taxable income, inflation, safety, or estate planning. The former business owner says, "I controlled my business, and now I can control my assets." The investment world, however, may well allow them less control than the business did.

QUESTIONS FOR REFLECTION AFTER THE SALE

Our staff at Oxbow has always done a good job of creating plans for 36 to 60 months. All former business owners are asked questions about their future vision and their appetite for risk. Listed below are a few examples of questions we often ask after a sale and some insight into why they should be considered.

- *Can you be employed by someone else and be happy?* The prospect of working for someone else is a sticky one for former business owners. Being the owner, boss, and ultimate decision maker is not a position easily exchanged for being subordinate to anyone. If going to work as an employee (even, or especially, for your former company) is not a possibility, it's better to recognize that fact right from the start.

- *Do you plan a change in family status?* This question takes many business owners by surprise, but everyone going through this process needs to take a moment to consider what we at Oxbow sometimes call the Ted Oakley $30 Million Question. We call it that because if you have a married couple walking away from a sale with $30 million after-tax community property, there is always a possibility one or both spouses will decide that after staying in the partnership while the couple worked together, built the company together, and raised a family together, they've had enough togetherness. This is a moment of reflection that may have been 20, 30, or 40 years in the making, and when it finally arrives, there is always a percentage who see it as the opportunity for a clean break.

- *Will you be moving?* And are you planning on dropping several million dollars on real estate? Relocation is always a big financial event and should be factored into investment decisions before any allocations for base capital and investment capital are made.

- *Have you made estate plans?* The arrival of a newly liquid fortune absolutely requires that families sit down together to consider their legacy plans. If your plans include making periodic gifts to the children in the near or long-term future, this also needs to be a factor in how you allocate your assets.

- *What has to happen over the next three years for you to feel good, both personally and financially?* You don't have to lay out everything you want to experience, but you will benefit from having a list of things you aspire to do and see. Consider it a work in progress. This is the perfect moment in your life to ask what you truly want next.

- *Will you start another business?* If so, how long do you intend to wait? At what level do you intend to be involved? How

YOU SOLD YOUR COMPANY

much of your newly liquid assets do you foresee investing in the new company? Your advising team does not want to tie up funds in long-term investments if you're going to want to tap them in a year or two to buy a company.

- *Where will your office be located?* Because unless you have strong convictions about plans that do not involve an office, we strongly suggest you get one. You don't have to have a 40-hour workweek to have an office. You just need to require a place to sequester yourself and consider business decisions. You may not be running the company anymore, but you are going to be overseeing the fate of a significant fortune, and that alone justifies having the sanctuary of an office space.

In most cases, business owners have focused on their companies, not their personal investments. By asking these and other very direct questions, we can start to get down to the core. What is this person's purpose? Is this person content? If not, why not?

Most business owners are working toward a goal or goals when the business is growing. They can usually recite sales goals, profit-and-loss information, and this month's numbers. But when asked about their personal investments and plans for next year, answers are in short supply. I often ask a question of business owners after the sale: "What exactly did you earn year to year on your investments?" I have yet to have a business owner give me a percentage return on his investments. Why? These individuals don't seem to realize that managing their money *is* their new business. It is still return on equity but now not in the business. It is still inventory turnover but now not in the business. It is still gross margins but now not in the business.

A plan will allow the former owner to think about each area. Cash flow, taxes, costs, pre-tax, and after-tax all still constitute factors in determining the big-picture plan.

DON'T FORGET TO LOOK BACK

The next part of the plan is to review after two or three years and determine to what extent the goals have been achieved. Adjustments often need to be made or goals changed. In order to invest for the future, more effort is needed than just meeting with four or five investment people and choosing one. What are their asset types? Which assets are bulletproof? Detailed thinking and analysis are important to investment health.

Most business owners are accustomed to paying themselves what they need while their business is private. After they sell, however, a great deal of thought is required in order to determine the amount of cash flow needed for living expenses. The risk factors associated with their investments need to be calculated, because of the need for consistent returns. Finally, consideration must be given to forecasting the capital requirements needed to start a new business—if that is the desire of the prior business owner. Unfortunately, these areas are often overlooked. They are much more important than most people realize.

Underestimating the value of planning is a classic mistake of former business owners. They tend to make nearly all of their decisions on a "have to" basis. The best approach is to have a steady flow of information and be prepared for all scenarios.

Given just how common this mistake is, I advise former business owners to be forgiving of their miscalculations and focused on the future in the first years after the sale. My friend and colleague Dan Sullivan has a great book called *The Gap and the Gain*, in which he advises against assessing accomplishments in terms of their position relative to the ideal—a practice that almost always leads to recognizing the gap between where you wanted to be and where you are. Instead, consider the gain: Where are you relative to where you were before?

From that point, you can turn your attention to making positive, productive plans for the next phase in your investment life.

OXBOW NOTE

In my book Your Money Mentality: How You Feel about Risk, Losses, and Gains, *I explain how investing is not linear and that successful investing sometimes goes against conventional wisdom. From my years of experience, I walk investors through the highs and lows of the market to help them determine their own money mentality. If you'd like a complimentary copy of this book, contact us at OxbowAdvisors.com.*

CHAPTER 17

Navigating the New Life

After selling a company, very few business owners have a road map for their immediate or long-term future. First of all, maps are hard to come by when you don't know your destination. Second, you need to ensure your assets and their income-producing power are sufficient to support you on your way.

ROAD MAP FACTOR #1: WHAT DIRECTION DO YOU CHOOSE?

Having great wealth doesn't change who you are, and it shouldn't change what matters most to you. What it does change is the freedom with which you can move through the world. If you don't want to go to work one morning (or ever again)? You have the freedom to do that. If you want to learn a new skill, see a new place, or start a new enterprise? You have the freedom to do that. If you want to leave a legacy or make a gift that will touch another person's life? That's also within your reach.

When you combine your newly liquid resources with the fact that you likely now have the luxury of time on your hands, there are few limits on what you can choose to do next.

One of your highest orders of business after the sale of your company is ensuring you will continue to have those options for the rest of your life.

Many former business owners have seldom stopped to consider what they'd do with total freedom. They were always busy building the company. So ask yourself: Now that I can do anything, what appeals to me?

Sometimes the answer is easy, like it was for Aaron, the 50-year-old owner of a textile business in the Southeast. He ran the company for 12 years and made a substantial profit at the time of selling the business. Prior to buying his original textile business, he had worked for a competing company. I visited with him on two occasions. After the second visit, I told him he would probably not be an investor with us. "Why do you say that?" he asked. My response was that it was clear that running his own company was his passion in life. I bet he'd buy another company and therefore need to keep his assets in cash or equivalents. Sure enough, it happened within two years.

Usually the seller's direction is not that obvious. Stu, for example, was a machine builder in the Midwest who had many patents in the company he sold. After the sale, I met with him and his wife and set up an investment plan for a secure and comfortable retirement. In the back of my mind, though, I had a hunch his insatiable appetite for building things wouldn't let him sit quietly by. He assured me this wasn't the case, so we put his money to work for a conservative future.

Within three years, Stu did indeed start a new company—under a schedule of four payments. Ultimately, we had to liquidate many of his investments for this business. After Stu's financial obligation was completed, he had very little liquidity left. He was fully aware of his new career and objectives (and their costs), and he was happy with them, but those long-term investments weren't the ideal path for him.

Other business owners know that retirement from day-to-day business is what they want. They want no employees, no payroll, no taxes, and no lawsuits. Bill is a fine person with whom I have done business for over 20 years. He moved to Florida after selling a company in another state. He loves every day, and he and his wife plan everything around their leisure and recreational activities. Leaving the business world completely behind was the perfect expression of what independence meant for him.

You don't have to (and in fact should not) plan out the rest of your life immediately after the sale of your company. But before you make major decisions that will impact how readily accessible your assets are in the long term, you should take some time to consider what potential major investments might be key to pursuing your idea of total freedom. With that in mind, you can make the right allocations for your base and investment capital.

ROAD MAP FACTOR #2: HOW WILL YOUR ASSETS SUPPORT THE LIFESTYLE?

The second main aspect of navigating the new life is size of assets and the power they hold. A business owner may take $200,000 to $600,000 per year for personal living expenditures out of the company and not even realize it. Most people don't fully appreciate the benefit of being able to produce large cash flows year after year. Very few business owners stop to think about what size of assets is needed to produce the income they'll want to replace after the sale.

At Oxbow, our experience has tracked certain characteristics of the different asset levels. Here are some thoughts about each:

- Business sales that generate between $5 million and $10 million can put former owners on a comfortable path, but most find they have to be more frugal than they expected in their lifestyle. For many, the reality is that the business produced far more cash flow than the assets ever will.

- After the sale of assets producing between $10 million and $20 million, the former owners will usually be able to produce a cash flow from investment income to equal their lifestyles as entrepreneurs. Even so, members of this group need to be prudent. If they make one or two sizable bad investments, their actual and emotional financial security may shift dramatically.

- Sellers who receive between $20 million and $50 million from the sale should have comfortable lives as long as they don't invest huge portions of their cash assets in one security—only to see it collapse in value before they can liquidate. Problems in this category usually arise when the individuals are concentrated in investments that are not well researched and analyzed. I have witnessed the fortunes of a number of people drop 75% or more because of a single risky investment.

- The sellers of company assets in the range of $50 million to $75 million are fewer in number and usually can absorb a couple of serious investment mistakes. The magnitude of their assets generally allows time for recovery, provided future investment decisions are conservative.

- The number of sellers who receive between $75 million and $250 million are fairly rare. At this level the sellers understand that taking risks is no longer necessary. What else can they buy? If they want more money, then it is the game that matters to them, not the wealth.

- Those sellers who receive between $250 million and $750 million for their companies are few and far between—and consequently can demand and pay for the best of services and goods. They know the power of their fortune, even if they downplay it. Many of them tend to make life very simple again.

- The owners of companies who liquidate for $750 million or above tend to be so private that information about them is hard to find. Discretion and security necessarily become very important to this group. Cash flow becomes a reverse problem. Where do they invest it?

When it comes down to it, of course, adequacy is always relative, and what constitutes "enough" is different for each person. Regardless of the size of the assets, the seller is advised to take time, keep a clear mind, and consider all facets of every major monetary decision. Do so from the very realistic perspective that what you are setting in motion will have long-term impacts on your financial future.

CHAPTER 18

Enjoy the Ride!

My personal observations about owners who sell companies are as follows: Business owners are the greatest group of people to work with in the world. They understand risk, reward, and achievement. Most all of them have had periods of high stress, serious setbacks, and great excitement. They are generally an optimistic lot, invariably believing that the positive will prevail. By and large, they are honest and endowed with high moral character. Entrepreneurial business owners are the true builders of this great country's economic foundation, the twin pillars of political and personal freedom. Unfortunately, business people seldom get much thanks for taking risks—and putting their personal savings and credit ratings on the line.

After they sell their companies, my wish for these individuals who have given much is enduring mental and financial security.

When counseling and managing investments for former business owners, we at Oxbow constantly emphasize the importance of peace of mind.

A WIDE-OPEN ROAD

When all the assets are transferred after the sale, in many ways you're back to square one in your life. You're looking around and deciding what you want to build and do and be in your next phase. It is my hope that some of the information in this book will help you consider which course is best.

In my experience, the people who do well in this critical period are well-rounded. They enjoy spending time with family. They are interested in making money, but it's not on their minds 24 hours a day. They're interested in topics outside their former industry. They are stable. And they are wise enough to be grateful.

The ones I see who go the other way may get the same amount of money, but their families rarely come first. They're always chasing something bigger and better. They compare themselves to others and covet what they don't have. They haven't figured out what makes them happy, so they're all about what they still "need" to become fulfilled. Of course, that never happens. The line is always moving, always a little out of reach.

There's a great book called *Solve for Happy* by Mo Gawdat, in which the author applies his considerable technical and intellectual skill to understanding the "formula" for happiness. Gawdat endured the unthinkable tragedy of losing his son, and his search for meaning afterward spurred his investigation. He concludes that happiness is equal to or greater than the events of your life—minus your expectations of how life should be. The theory applies to nearly every wealthy individual I've met, regardless of the sums and circumstances. Some are perfectly content for the rest of their lives with modest fortunes. Some maintain expectations that are always higher than the world can deliver. There are individuals out there in their 80s and older with hundreds of millions in the bank who are still striving for whatever they didn't get. Their fortunes aren't big enough. Their kids aren't good enough. The recognition they've received for their accomplishments always comes up short.

There are times when I wonder if anyone has ever posed the seemingly obvious question to them: *You do know you're going to die, don't you? Wouldn't you like to enjoy your life a little bit first?*

It's possible they could do it simply by adjusting their expectations enough to be able to appreciate what they have.

A DIFFERENT KIND OF INVESTMENT

In my opinion, success lies in knowing you did the best you could do with the tools and resources available. A lifetime teacher who touches the lives of many hundreds of children is just as successful as Sam Walton of Walmart. Who is to say that dollars or net worth are the only benchmarks of a successful and well-lived life?

Over the last 30 or so years, I have seen former business owners render all kinds of personal services for others, enhancing their own lives in the process. One of my client friends in North Carolina helped his housekeeper and her church by paying off the congregation's debt. Another client in California lends a hand to assist people in his life in achieving their goals (everyone from his personal employees to high school friends to individuals he meets in his community).

Jack was a fantastic businessman who sold his company, then set up foundations and charitable channels of all sorts. He was a tough guy to deal with, but he had a truly generous heart. He contributed money to great causes and never once looked for recognition. The ability to help people was what Jack most enjoyed and what gave his life the most meaning.

My good friend and mentor, Frank Knapp Jr., who helped me write this book, has always said that helping people while you can see them benefit in life is much more rewarding than bequests after death. Most former owners of businesses practice this in some form. They give to people quietly, without needing recognition or fanfare. I can attest that in December of each year my staff is inundated with directives from clients to transfer money to charities. Those requests come from people who are giving back something they feel was given to them.

Having net worth allows an individual the ability to help others and thus gain a stronger sense of self-worth. The returns on these investments may not always be quantifiable, but they are undeniable. They help bring purpose in life more sharply into focus. The seller's new world of liquidity offers meaningful opportunities to invest in others, to help them reach their potential, and to encourage them to build their sense of self-worth by contributing to their own success. Carefully considering the best ways to help others becomes, for some, a vocation. For many former business owners, it turns out this rewarding work essentially *is* the next business—one that may become their most lasting legacy.

In the end, your life's journey is just a ride, and success is just one part of that. A hundred years from now, all that will remain of each of us will be a tombstone with two dates. In the block of time between them, you may get 70 years, or 90, or 100. Now that you've worked your way to this unique stretch of independence, how do you want to spend your time? Think about it, and do it, before it's too late.

Build the business. Sell the business. Start over. Retire. Start giving. Start your next adventure. There are endless possibilities. Whatever you do, enjoy the ride!

Acknowledgments

I'm reminded of the insightful words of a woman named Sandra Carey. She said, "Never mistake knowledge for wisdom. One helps you make a living; the other helps you make a life."

I am greatly indebted to many individuals who have helped me along my way. I want to express my heartfelt gratitude to all the business owners I've known—and whose knowledge and wisdom have served as the road map for this book.

Many thanks to those who have helped me with this endeavor, including Frank Knapp Jr., Keys Oakley, Nancy Brazzil Oakley, Dan Kennedy, and Jana Murphy.

Should you read this book and sell your company sometime in the future, I hope the information you found here will be helpful. If you have already sold, may you—and those whose lives you touch—enjoy the fruits of your labors.

—Ted Oakley, January 2022

About the Author

J. TED OAKLEY, founder and managing partner of Oxbow Advisors, began his career in the investment industry in 1976. The Oxbow Principles and the firm's proprietary investment strategies are founded on the unique perspective he has gained during his decades-long tenure advising high-net-worth investors. Ted's investment advice provides principled guidance to investors from more than 40 US states. He frequently counsels former business owners on protecting and wisely investing their newly liquid wealth.

Ted is the author of several other books, including:

$20 Million and Broke: If You Have It, Don't Lose It

Your Money Mentality: How You Feel about Risk, Losses, and Gains

The Psychology of Staying Rich: How to Preserve Wealth and Establish an Enduring Financial Legacy

Crazy Time: Surviving the First 12 Months after Selling Your Company

Danger Time: The Two-Year Red Zone after Selling Your Company

Rich Kids, Broke Kids: The Failure of Traditional Estate Planning

Wall Street Lies: 5 Myths to Keep Your Cash in Their Game (with Pat Swanson and Trey Crain)

My Story

www.ingramcontent.com/pod-product-compliance
Lightning Source LLC
Chambersburg PA
CBHW071702210326
41597CB00017B/2289